Bonhoeffer for a New Generation

BONHOEFFER
for a New Generation

Edited by Otto Dudzus

SCM PRESS LTD

Extracts taken from
The Cost of Discipleship translated by R. H. Fuller, © SCM
Press 1948, 1959; *Ethics* translated by Neville Horton
Smith, © SCM Press 1955; *Letters and Papers from Prison*
translated by R. H. Fuller, Frank Clark and John
Bowden, © SCM Press 1953, 1967, 1971; *Life Together*
translated by John W. Doberstein, © Harper and Row
1954; *No Rusty Swords, The Way to Freedom* and *True
Patriotism* (vols I, II and III of selections from *Gesammelte
Schriften*) translated by Edwin H. Robertson and John
Bowden, © Collins and Harper and Row 1965, 1966,
1973. Additional hitherto untranslated material from
Gesammelte Schriften I and II, Christian Kaiser ³1978, ²1965
and *Predigten* I and II, Christian Kaiser 1984, 1985,
translation © John Bowden 1986.

British Library Cataloguing in Publication Data

Bonhoeffer, Dietrich
Bonhoeffer for a new generation
1. Christian life
I. Title II. Dudzus, Otto III. Dietrich
Bonhoeffer Lesebuch. *English*
248.4   BV4501.2

ISBN 0-334-00130-7

First published in Britain 1986
by SCM Press Ltd
26-30 Tottenham Road, London N1 4BZ

Photoset by Input Typesetting Ltd, London
and printed in Great Britain by
Richard Clay (The Chaucer Press) Ltd
Bungay, Suffolk

Contents

Preface

This book seeks to present to a wider audience important passages from the writings of Dietrich Bonhoeffer which are scattered throughout a variety of publications. They come from all periods of his activity. By far the majority of them are taken from the writings which made him especially well known: *The Cost of Discipleship*, *Life Together*, *Ethics* and *Letters and Papers from Prison*. Gathered together here, they aim at providing a general impression of Bonhoeffer's person and work.

Common to almost all Bonhoeffer's books is that they were written in connection with a situation where a quite specific decision had to be taken. *The Cost of Discipleship* was written when the Protestant Church in Germany was fighting for its survival and needed to recover its foundations. The fragments which make up *Ethics* were produced when the church became excessively preoccupied with its struggle for survival and in so doing restricted the range of the Lordship of Christ, obscured the fact that he is there for all oppressed and ill-treated humanity, and threatened to deny his significance for the rule of truth and justice in public life. And *Letters and Papers from Prison* is full of new theological perspectives which are closely connected with the decisions which Bonhoeffer himself had to respond to or to make. That is the reason why Bonhoeffer's works still evoke a lasting response wherever they are read and why even forty years after his death they are constantly found relevant for decisions which have to be made in the present time.

First of all in this book comes the poem 'Stations on the Road to Freedom'. It serves, so to speak, as an overture which contains all the themes to be developed later. One stroke of luck which helps towards an authentic interpretation of Bonhoeffer is that at a time when he had to expect his own imminent death – after the failure of the attempt to overthrow Hitler on 20 July 1944 – he once again set down the motives which dominated his whole life in a kind of miniature and extremely concentrated biography. In the end, even Eberhard Bethge's great biography does not in fact do more than describe how all his life Bonhoeffer was in search of a freedom – for himself and others – which has deep roots, which is convincing, and which cannot be limited by suffering and death. And it is clear that in every instance Bonhoeffer could only find this freedom in seeking constant conformity to the figure of Christ. Where else could it be found? Following Christ, being a disciple, became the one great theme of his life. He had to prove his discipleship in very different spheres of life, some of them ordinary and later some quite extraordinary. He did not seek out the unusual ones for himself. But he knew that he could not avoid them at any price because of what he had come to know of Christ.

All this means that Bonhoeffer's life work is a unity. There can be no question of playing the 'early' Bonhoeffer off against the 'late', the 'pious' Bonhoeffer against the 'religionless', the 'conservative' Bonhoeffer against the 'revolutionary'. Bonhoeffer himself provided the strongest arguments against such one-sided and divisive interpretations in his 'Stations on the Road to Freedom'. Is it quite unjustified to hope that in the present confrontations within Christianity in so many countries of the world, where those who cling anxiously to positions and insights formerly gained oppose those who are going forward in hope on the road to justice, freedom and peace opened up by Christ, we can begin from the reconciliatory initiatives pioneered by Bonhoeffer? There are not many people with such powers of integration.

September 1985   Otto Dudzus

STATIONS ON THE ROAD TO FREEDOM

Discipline

If you set out to seek freedom, then learn above all things
to govern your soul and your senses, for fear that your passions
and longing may lead you away from the path you should follow,
Chaste be your mind and your body, and both in subjection,
obediently, steadfastly seeking the aim set before them;
only through discipline may a man learn to be free.

Action

Daring to do what is right, not what fancy may tell you,
valiantly grasping occasions, not cravenly doubting –
freedom comes only through deeds, not through thoughts taking
    wing.
Faint not nor fear, but go out to the storm and the action,
trusting in God whose commandment you faithfully follow;
freedom, exultant, will welcome your spirit with joy.

Suffering

A change has come indeed. Your hands, so strong and active,
are bound: in helplessness now you see your action
is ended; you sigh in relief, your cause committing
to stronger hands; so now you may rest contented.
Only for one blissful moment could you draw near to touch
    freedom;
then, that it might be perfected in glory, you gave it to God.

Death

Come now, thou greatest of feasts on the journey to freedom
   eternal;
death, cast aside all the burdensome chains, and demolish
the walls of our temporal body, the walls of our souls that are
   blinded,
so that at last we may see that which here remains hidden.
Freedom, how long we have sought thee in discipline, action,
   and suffering;
dying, we now may behold thee revealed in the Lord.

Letters and Papers from Prison, 370f.

I · DISCIPLINE

Introduction

The title of this first section has somewhat ominous overtones for us. We have become too used to thinking in a way which regards terms like order and discipline simply as opposites to freedom, a limitation to, if not an endangering of, full humanity.

Bonhoeffer can teach us better. By discipline he understands asking about and search for the laws under which life can first develop and flourish, the mystery which determines whether life succeeds or is lost. Here discipline has a wide range. It is not bound up with a particular phase of development, and no sphere of our life escapes it.

That includes quite simple things which seem to us to be almost too trivial. In his letter of 18 December 1943 from prison Bonhoeffer wrote how important it was not to have any disorder in the course of his day. That would be the beginning of capitulation 'and worse would probably have followed. An outward and purely physical regime (exercises and a cold wash down in the morning) itself provides some support for one's inner discipline' (*Letters and Papers from Prison*, 168).

We find this inner discipline described in more detail in his small piece 'The Morning'. 'Bad temper, uncontrolled moods and wishes which we cannot get rid of during the day often come to haunt us at night, as ghosts which cannot be exorcised and which seek to embitter our days. Our own plans and concerns do not belong in the first moments of the new day, nor does an excessive zeal for work, but God's liberating grace, the blessing of God's presence' (*Predigten* II, 186). Bonhoeffer was more afraid of inner chaos than anything else. He was aware that collapse here was closely connected with a collapse into chaos in major matters, with

3

our susceptibility to it, our helplessness in the face of it. And above all he knew that the most effective help against both inward and outward chaos lies in patient, faithful listening to the word of God and doing his will. To this degree, for Bonhoeffer, following Christ is simply another word for discipline.

The inner order gained through discipleship is tested in our relationships with other people, those nearest to us and those furthest away. Bonhoeffer has left us an extraordinarily fine and helpful account of this in his *Life Together*. From it come most of the passages which concern this sphere of our life. How we can gain access to other people; how we have to reflect them in their mystery; what community is; the relationship between being together and being alone, each being a person in his or her own right yet depending on one another, relating to one another; how speaking and being silent belong together and affect each other – all this can be found here in passages which have almost become classics. In this context also belongs the sermon on peace that Bonhoeffer gave at the 1934 Fanö conference, in which these issues are transferred to the major areas of life. What he said then about peace in the world is only now beginning to be fully realized and to have an influence.

'From the poverty and pettiness of our own little convictions and problems, we seek wealth and splendour which are vouchsafed to us in Jesus Christ' wrote Bonhoeffer in 1937 in the introduction to *The Cost of Discipleship*. The last passages in this section show what mature results can grow out of such a search for a personal life-style. They are all taken from Bonhoeffer's letters from prison and are only a small selection from what could have been quoted. One might expect that the conditions of prison, which otherwise are only inflicted on serious criminals, would remove all possibilities of openness and freedom. But the letters show that Bonhoeffer never showed openness and freedom as convincingly as he does here. He not only talks about them, but actually lives them out in an impressive way.

O.D.

Cheap grace is the deadly enemy of our church. We are fighting today for costly grace.

Cheap grace means grace sold on the market like cheapjack's wares. The sacraments, the forgiveness of sin, and the consolations of religion are thrown away at cut prices. Grace is represented as the church's inexhaustible treasury, from which she showers blessings with generous hands, without asking questions or fixing limits. Grace without price; grace without cost! The essence of grace, we suppose, is that the account has been paid in advance; and, because it has been paid, everything can be had for nothing. Since the cost was infinite, the possibilities of using and spending it are infinite. What would grace be if it were not cheap? . . .

Costly grace is the gospel which must be *sought* again and again, the gift which must be *asked* for, the door at which a man must *knock*.

Such grace is *costly* because it calls us to follow, and it is *grace* because it calls us to follow *Jesus Christ*. It is costly because it costs a man his life, and it is grace because it gives a man the only true life. It is costly because it condemns sin, and grace because it justifies the sinner . . . Costly grace is the Incarnation of God . . .

As Christianity spread, and the church became more secularized, this realization of the costliness of grace gradually faded. The world was Christianized, and grace became its common property. It was to be had at low cost. Yet the Church of Rome did not altogether lose the earlier vision. It is highly significant that the church was astute enough to find room for the monastic movement, and to prevent it from lapsing into schism. Here on the outer fringe of the church was a place where the older vision was kept alive. Here men still remembered that grace costs, that grace means following Christ. Here they left all they had for Christ's sake, and endeavoured daily to practise his rigorous commands. Thus monasticism became a living protest against the secularization of Christianity and the cheapening of grace . . . The fatal error of monasticism lay not so much in its rigorism . . . as in the extent to which it departed from genuine Christianity by

5

setting up itself as the individual achievement of a select few, and so claiming a special merit of its own.

When the Reformation came, the providence of God raised Martin Luther to restore the gospel of pure, costly grace. Luther passed through the cloister; he was a monk, and all this was part of the divine plan. Luther had left all to follow Christ on the path of absolute obedience. He had renounced the world in order to live the Christian life. He had learnt obedience to Christ and to his church, because only he who is obedient can believe. The call to the cloister demanded of Luther the complete surrender of his life. But God shattered all his hopes. He showed him through the scriptures that the following of Christ is not the achievement or merit of a select few, but the divine command to all Christians without distinction . . .

Luther's return from the cloister to the world was the worst blow the world had suffered since the days of early Christianity. The renunciation he made when he became a monk was child's play compared with that which he had to make when he returned to the world. Now came the frontal assault. The only way to follow Jesus was by living in the world. Hitherto the Christian life had been the achievement of a few choice spirits under the exceptionally favourable conditions of monasticism; now it is a duty laid on every Christian living in the world. The commandment of Jesus must be accorded perfect obedience in one's daily vocation of life . . .

It is a fatal misunderstanding of Luther's action to suppose that his rediscovery of the gospel of pure grace offered a general dispensation from obedience to the command of Jesus, or that it was the great discovery of the Reformation that God's forgiving grace automatically conferred upon the world both righteousness and holiness. On the contrary, for Luther the Christian's worldly calling is sanctified only in so far as that calling registers the final, radical protest against the world. Only in so far as the Christian's secular calling is exercised in the following of Jesus does it receive from the gospel new sanction and justification. It was not the justification of sin, but the justification of the sinner that drove Luther from the cloister back into the world. The grace he had received was costly grace. It was grace, for it was like water on parched ground, comfort in tribulation, freedom from the bondage of a self-chosen way, and forgiveness of all his sins. And it was costly, for, so far from dispensing him from good works, it meant that he must take the call to discipleship more seriously than ever before. It was grace because it cost so much and it cost so much because it was grace. That was the secret of the gospel of the Reformation – the justification of the sinner.

The Cost of Discipleship, 35–41

The morning

Each new day is a new beginning in our life. Each day is a self-contained whole. Today is the limit of our cares and concerns (Matt. 6.34; James 4.14). Today is long enough to find God or to lose him, to keep the faith or to succumb to sin and shame. God created day and night so that we should not wander in boundless space but in the morning already see before us our evening's destination. Just as the old sun is new each day it rises, so too the eternal mercy of God is new every morning (Lam. 3.23). To understand God's old faithfulness anew every morning, to be able to begin a new life with God in the midst of a life with God, is the gift that God gives us every morning.

In the Bible the morning is a time full of wonder. It is the time when God helps his church (Ps. 46.6), the time of joy after a night of weeping (Ps. 30.6), the hour for the proclamation of the word of God (Zeph. 3.5), of the daily distribution of the sacred manna (Ex. 16.13f.). Jesus gets up to pray before daybreak, and in the early morning the women go to the tomb and find Jesus risen (Mark 16.2ff.). In the first light of day the disciples find the Risen Christ on the shore of the Sea of Galilee (John 21.4). It is the expectation of the miracle of God which makes the men of faith rise early (Gen. 19.27; Ex. 24.4; Job 1.5 etc.). Sleep no longer holds them. They hasten to meet God's early grace.

When we wake we can drive away the dark shades of night and the confusions of our dreams by immediately uttering the morning blessing and commending ourselves on this day to the help of the triune God. Bad temper, uncontrolled moods and wishes which we cannot get rid of during the day often come to haunt us at night, as ghosts which cannot be exorcised and which seek to embitter our days. Our own plans and concerns do not belong in the first moments of the new day, nor does an excessive zeal for work, but God's liberating grace, the blessing of God's presence. Anyone who is woken early by anxiety is told by scripture, 'It is vain that you rise up early and go late to rest, eating the bread of anxious toil' (Ps. 127.2). It is not anxiety about the day, the burden of the work that I plan to do, but the Lord who 'wakens me morning by morning; he wakens my ear to hear as those who are taught', as is said of the servant of God (Isa. 50.4). Before the heart opens itself to the world it must open itself to God. Before the ear perceives the countless voices of the day it must listen in the early morning to the voice of the creator and redeemer. God has prepared the stillness of the earliest morning for himself. It must belong to him.

The daily word belongs before daily bread. Only in this way will we receive our bread with thanksgiving. Morning prayer belongs before daily work. Only in this way is work done in fulfilment of the divine commandment. The morning must provide an hour for quiet prayer and shared reflection. This is truly not a waste of time. How else can we equip ourselves to meet the tasks, the needs and the demands of the day? And while we may not often be in the mood for it, it is a service we owe the one whose will it is to be called on, praised and prayed to by us, the one who wants to bless our day for us simply through his word and our prayer.

It is not a good thing to talk of 'legalism' in connection with the ordering of our Christian life, with the faithfulness in the reading of scripture and prayer that are enjoined on us. Disorder makes faith disintegrate and shatter. That is a lesson to be learned above all by the theologian who confuses indiscipline with the freedom of the gospel. Anyone who is responsible for a demanding spiritual ministry and does not want to lose himself and his work in a flurry of activity must also learn the spiritual discipline of the servant of Jesus Christ. The young theologian will find it a great help to set aside fixed times for silent prayer and meditation to be kept persistently and patiently.

Every Christian needs a time of silent prayer. The theologian who wants to be a Christian needs it more than anyone else. He needs more time for the word of God and for prayer, for that is his particular task (Acts 6.4). How can we learn to deal with God's word through the day, preach and teach, help to bear one another's burdens in brotherhood, if we have not ourselves experienced God's help for the day? We should not become chatterers and know-alls. It is advisable to base our time of silent prayer on a word of God. That gives our prayer content, a firm foundation, and confidence. We can use the same passage of the Bible for a week. Then the Word will begin to dwell in us and live in us and thus be present in us, consciously or unconsciously. If we change too quickly the passage we use for meditation, we shall become superficial. On the basis of scripture we learn to speak to God in the language in which God has spoken to us, like a child talking to its father. Starting from the Word of God we pray all that the word teaches us; we bring the coming day before God and purify our ideas and plans before him; we pray above all for the full communion of Jesus Christ with us. We should not forget to pray for ourselves: 'In humility, hold your head high' (Sirach 11.1).

Then we have the broad fields of intercession. Here our horizons are broadened. We see people and things, near and far, who need to be commended to the grace of God. No one who has asked for our prayers should be left out. And in addition there are all those who are particularly close to us, personally or in their calling – and there will be many of them. Finally, we all know people who are unlikely to be prayed for unless we pray for them. Nor should we forget to thank God for those who help and strengthen us through their intercessions. We should not bring our time of silent prayer to an end before we have said the Amen often, and finally with great certainty.

Now God has spoken his word in the silence of the morning: now we have found communion with him and with the community of Christians. Is that not enough to enable us to go confidently to our daily work?

1935 or 1936
Predigten II, 185–9

The hiddenness of prayer

Jesus teaches his disciples to pray. What does this mean? It means that prayer is by no means an obvious or natural activity. It is the expression of a universal human instinct, but that does not justify it in the sight of God. Even where prayer is cultivated with discipline and perseverence it can still be profitless and void of God's blessing. The disciples are permitted to pray because Jesus tells them they may – and he knows the Father. He promises that God will hear them. That is to say, the disciples pray only because they are followers of Christ and have fellowship with him. Only those who, like them, adhere to Jesus have access to the Father through him. All Christian prayer is directed to God through a Mediator, and not even prayer affords direct access to the Father. Only through Jesus Christ can we find the Father in prayer. Christian prayer presupposes faith, that is, adherence to Christ. He is the one and only Mediator of our prayers. We pray at his command, and to that word Christian prayer is always bound.

We pray to God because we believe in him through Jesus Christ; that is to say, our prayer can never be an entreaty to God, for we have no need to come before him in that way. We are privileged to know that he knows our needs before we ask him. This is what gives Christian prayer its boundless confidence and its joyous certainty. It matters little what form of prayer we adopt or how many words we use, what matters is the faith which lays hold on God and touches the heart of the Father who knew us long before we came to him.

Genuine prayer is never 'good works', an exercise or a pious attitude, but it is always the prayer of a child to a Father. Hence it is never given to self-display, whether before God, ourselves, or other people. If God were ignorant of our needs, we should have to think out beforehand *how* we should tell him about them, *what* we should tell him, and whether we should tell him or not. Thus faith, which is the mainspring of Christian prayer, excludes all reflection and premeditation.

Prayer is the supreme instance of the hidden character of the Christian life. It is the antithesis of self-display. When men pray, they have ceased to know themselves, and know only God whom they call upon. Prayer does not aim at any direct effect on the world; it is addressed to God alone, and is therefore the perfect example of undemonstrative action.

Of course there is a danger even here. Prayer of this kind can seek self-display, it can seek to bring to light that which is hidden.

This may happen in public prayer, which sometimes (though not often nowadays) degenerates into an empty noise. But there is no difference; it is even more pernicious if I turn myself into a spectator of my own prayer performance, if I am giving a show for my own benefit. I may enjoy myself just like a pleased spectator or I may catch myself praying and feel strange and ashamed. The publicity of the market place affords only a more naïve form than the publicity which I am providing for myself. I can lay on a very nice show for myself even in the privacy of my own room. That is the extent to which we can distort the word of Jesus. The publicity which I am looking for is then provided by the fact that I am the one who at the same time prays and looks on. I am listening to my own prayer and thus I am answering my own prayer. Not being content to wait for God to answer our prayer and show us in his own time that he has heard us, we provide our own answer. We take note that we have prayed suitably well, and this substitutes the satisfaction of answered prayer. We have our reward. Since we have heard ourselves, God will not hear us. Having contrived our own reward of publicity, we cannot expect God to reward us any further.

Where is the innermost chamber Jesus is thinking of where I can hide, if I cannot be sure of myself? How can I lock it so well that no audience spoils the anonymity of prayer and thus robs me of the reward of hidden prayer? How are we to be protected from ourselves, and our own premeditations? How are we to drive out reflection by reflecting? The only way is by mortifying our own wills which are always obtruding themselves. And the only way to do this is by letting Christ alone reign in our hearts, by surrendering our wills completely to him, by living in fellowship with Jesus and by following him. Then we can pray that his will may be done, the will of him who knows our needs before we ask. Only then is our prayer certain, strong and pure. And then prayer is really and truly *petition*. The child asks of the Father whom he knows. Thus the essence of Christian prayer is not general adoration, but definite, concrete petition. The right way to approach God is to stretch out our hands and ask of One who we know has the heart of a Father.

True prayer is done in secret, but this does not rule out the fellowship of prayer altogether, however clearly we may be aware

11

of its dangers. In the last resort it is immaterial whether we pray in the open street or in the secrecy of our chambers, whether briefly or lengthily, in the litany of the church, or with the sigh of one who knows not what he should pray for. True prayer does not depend either on the individual or the whole body of the faithful, but solely upon the knowledge that our heavenly Father knows our needs. That makes God the sole object of our prayers, and frees us from a false confidence in our own prayerful efforts.

The Cost of Discipleship, 145–147

Not being ashamed

Meanwhile we've had the expected large-scale attack on Borsig. It really is a strange feeling, to see the 'Christmas trees', the flares that the leading aircraft drops, coming down right over our heads. The shouting and screaming of the prisoners in their cells was terrible. We had no dead, only injured, and we had finished bandaging them by one o'clock. After that, I was able to drop off at once into a sound sleep. People here talk quite openly about how frightened they were. I don't quite know what to make of it, for fright is surely something to be ashamed of. I have a feeling that it shouldn't be talked about except in the confessional, otherwise it might easily involve a certain amount of exhibitionism; and *a fortiori* there is no need to play the hero. On the other hand, naïve frankness can be quite disarming. But even so, there's a cynical, I might almost say ungodly, frankness, the kind that breaks out in heavy drinking and fornication, and gives the impression of chaos. I wonder whether fright is not one of the *pudenda*, which ought to be concealed. I must think about it further.

I've been thinking again over what I wrote to you recently about our own fear. I think that here, under the guise of honesty, something is being passed off as 'natural' that is at bottom a symptom of sin; it is really quite analogous to talking openly about sexual matters. After all, 'truthfulness' does not mean uncovering everything that exists. God himself made clothes for men; and that means that *in statu corruptionis* many things in human life ought to remain covered, and that evil, even though it cannot be

12

eradicated, ought at least to be concealed. Exposure is cynical, and although the cynic prides himself on his exceptional honesty, or claims to want truth at all costs, he misses the crucial fact that since the fall there must be reticence and secrecy. In my opinion the greatness of Stifter lies in his refusal to force his way into man's inner life, in his respect for reticence, and in his willingness to observe people more or less cautiously from the outside but not from the inside. Inquisitiveness is alien to him. I remember once being impressed when Frau von Kleist-Kieckow told me with genuine horror about a film that showed the growth of a plant speeded up; she said that she and her husband could not stand it, as they felt it to be an impermissible prying into the mystery of life. Stifter takes a similar line. But is not this somewhat akin to the so-called English 'hypocrisy', which we contrast with German 'honesty'? I believe we Germans have never properly grasped the meaning of 'concealment', i.e. what is in the end the *status corruptionis* of the world. Kant says quite rightly in his *Anthropologie* that anyone who misunderstands or questions the significance of outward appearance in the world is a traitor to humanity.

27 November and 5 December 1943
Letters and Papers from Prison, 146, 158

Keeping pace with God

When *we* are forcibly separated for any considerable time from those whom we love, we simply *cannot*, as most can, get some cheap substitute through other people – I don't mean because of moral considerations, but just because we are what we are. Substitutes repel us; we simply have to wait and wait; we have to suffer unspeakably from the separation, and feel the longing till it almost makes us ill. That is the only way, although it is a very painful one, in which we can preserve unimpaired our relationship with our loved ones. A few times in my life I've come to know what homesickness means. There is nothing more painful, and during these months in prison I've sometimes been terribly home-sick. And as I expect you will have to go through the same kind of thing in the coming months I wanted to write and tell you what I've learnt about it; in case it may be of some help to you. The first result of such longing is always a wish to neglect the ordinary daily routine in some way or other, and that means that our lives become disordered. I used to be tempted sometimes to stay in bed after six in the morning (it would have been perfectly possible), and to sleep on. Up to now I've always been able to force myself not to do this; I realized that it would have been the first stage of capitulation, and that worse would probably have followed. An outward and purely physical régime (exercises and a cold wash down in the morning) itself provides some support for one's inner discipline. Further, there is nothing worse in such times than to try to find a substitute for the irreplaceable. It just does not work, and it leads to still greater indiscipline, for the strength to overcome tension (such strength can come only from looking the longing straight in the face) is impaired, and endurance becomes even more unbearable . . .

Another point: I don't think it is good to talk to strangers about our condition; that always stirs up one's troubles – although we ought to be ready, when occasion arises, to listen to those of other people. Above all, we must never give way to self-pity. And on the Christian aspect of the matter, there are some lines that say

> . . . that we remember what we would forget,
> that this poor earth is not our home.

That is indeed something essential, but it must come last of all. I believe that we ought so to love and trust God in our *lives*, and in all the good things that he sends us, that when the time comes (but not before!) we may go to him with love, trust, and joy. But, to put it plainly, for a man in his wife's arms to be hankering after the other world is, in mild terms, a piece of bad taste, and not God's will. We ought to find and love God in what he actually gives us; if it pleases him to allow us to enjoy some overwhelming earthly happiness, we mustn't try to be more pious than God himself and allow our happiness to be corrupted by presumption and arrogance, and by unbridled religious fantasy which is never satisfied with what God gives. God will see to it that the man who finds him in his earthly happiness and thanks him for it does not lack reminder that earthly things are transient, that it is good for him to attune his heart to what is eternal, and that sooner or later there will be times when he can say in all sincerity, 'I wish I were home.' But everything has its time, and the main thing is that we keep step with God, and do not keep pressing on a few steps ahead – nor keep dawdling a step behind. It's presumptuous to want to have everything at once – matrimonial bliss, the cross, and the heavenly Jerusalem, where they neither marry nor are given in marriage. 'For everything there is a season' (Eccles. 3.1); everything has its time: 'a time to weep, and a time to laugh; . . . a time to embrace, and a time to refrain from embracing; . . . a time to rend, and a time to sew; . . . and God seeks again what is past.' I suspect that these last words mean that nothing that is past is lost, that God gathers up again with us our past, which belongs to us. So when we are seized by a longing for the past – and this may happen when we least expect it – we may be sure that it is only one of the many 'hours' that God is always holding ready for us. So we oughtn't to seek the past again by our own efforts, but only with God.

18 December 1943
Letters and Papers from Prison, 167ff.

Through Christ to our brothers

It is not simply to be taken for granted that the Christian has the privilege of living among other Christians. Jesus Christ lived in the midst of his enemies. At the end all his disciples deserted him. On the cross he was utterly alone, surrounded by evildoers and mockers. For this cause he had come, to bring peace to the enemies of God. So the Christian, too, belongs not in the seclusion of a cloistered life but in the thick of foes. There is his commission, his work. 'The Kingdom is to be in the midst of your enemies. And he who will not suffer this does not want to be of the Kingdom of Christ; he wants to be among friends, to sit among roses and lilies, not with the bad people but the devout people. O you blasphemers and betrayers of Christ! If Christ had done what you are doing who would ever have been spared?' (Luther) . . .

So between the death of Christ and the Last Day it is only by a gracious anticipation of the last things that Christians are privileged to live in visible fellowship with other Christians. It is by the grace of God that a congregation is permitted to gather visibly in

15

this world to share God's Word and sacrament. Not all Christians receive this blessing . . .

The physical presence of other Christians is a source of incomparable joy and strength to the believer . . .

The believer feels no shame, as though he were still living too much in the flesh, when he yearns for the physical presence of other Christians. Man was created a body, the Son of God appeared on earth in the body, he was raised in the body, in the sacrament the believer receives the Lord Christ in the body, and the resurrection of the dead will bring about the perfected fellowship of God's spiritual-physical creatures. The believer therefore lauds the Creator, the Redeemer, God, Father, Son and Holy Spirit, for the bodily presence of a brother . . .

Christianity means community through Jesus Christ and in Jesus Christ. No Christian community is more or less than this. Whether it be a brief, single encounter or the daily fellowship of years. Christian community is only this. We belong to one another only through and in Jesus Christ . . .

The Christian is the man who no longer seeks his salvation, his deliverance, his justification in himself, but in Jesus Christ alone. He knows that God's Word in Jesus Christ pronounces him guilty, even when he does not feel his guilt, and God's Word in Jesus Christ pronounces him not guilty and righteous, even when he does not feel that he is righteous at all. The Christian no longer lives of himself, by his own claims and his own justification, but by God's claims and God's justification. He lives wholly by God's Word pronounced upon him, whether that Word declares him guilty or innocent.

The death and the life of the Christian is not determined by his own resources; rather he finds both only in the Word that comes to him from the outside, in God's Word to him. The Reformers expressed it this way: Our righteousness is an 'alien righteousness', a righteousness that comes from outside of us (*extra nos*). They were saying that the Christian is dependent on the Word of God spoken to him. He is pointed outward, to the Word that comes to him. The Christian lives wholly by the truth of God's Word in Jesus Christ. If somebody asks him, Where is your salvation, your righteousness? he can never point to himself. He points to the Word of God in Jesus Christ, which assures him salvation and righteousness. He is as alert as possible to this Word. Because he daily hungers and thirsts for righteousness, he daily desires the redeeming Word. And it can come only from the outside. In himself he is destitute and dead. Help must come from the outside, and it has come and comes daily and anew in the Word of Jesus Christ, bringing redemption, righteousness, innocence, and blessedness.

But God has put this Word into the mouth of men in order that it may be communicated to other men. When one person is struck by the Word, he speaks it to others. God has willed that we should seek him and find his living Word in the witness of a brother, in the mouth of a man. Therefore, a Christian needs another Christian who speaks God's Word to him. He needs him again and again when he becomes uncertain and discouraged, for by himself he cannot help himself without belying the truth. He needs his brother man as a bearer and proclaimer of the divine word of salvation. He needs his brother solely because of Jesus Christ. The Christ in his own heart is weaker than the Christ in the word of his brother; his own heart is uncertain, his brother's is sure.

And that also clarifies the goal of all Christian community: they meet one another as bringers of the message of salvation. As such, God permits them to meet together and gives them community . . .

A Christian comes to others only through Jesus Christ. Among men there is strife. 'He is our peace', says Paul of Jesus Christ (Eph. 2.14). Without Christ there is discord between God and man and between man and man. Christ became the Mediator and made peace with God and among men. Without Christ we should not know God and could not call upon him, nor come to him. But without Christ we would also not know our brother, nor could we come to him. The way is blocked by our own ego. Christ opened up the way to God and to our brother. Now Christians can live with one another in peace; they can love and serve one another; they can become one. But they can continue to do so only by way of Jesus Christ. Only in Jesus Christ are we one, only through him are we bound together. To eternity he remains the one Mediator . . .

One is a brother to another only through Jesus Christ. I am a brother to another person through what Jesus Christ did for me

17

and to me; the other person has become a brother to me through what Jesus Christ did for him. This fact that we are brethren only through Jesus Christ is of immeasurable significance. Not only the other person who is earnest and devout, who comes to me seeking brotherhood, must I deal with in fellowship. My brother is rather that other person who has been redeemed by Christ, delivered from sin, and called to faith and eternal life. Not what a man is in himself as a Christian, his spirituality and piety, constitutes the basis of our community. What determines our brotherhood is what that man is by reason of Christ. Our community with one another consists solely in what Christ has done to both of us. This is true not merely at the beginning, as though in the course of time something else were to be added to our community; it remains so for all the future and to all eternity. I have community with others and I shall continue to have it only through Jesus Christ. The more genuine and the deeper our community becomes, the more will everything else between us recede, the more clearly and purely will Jesus Christ and his work become the one and only thing that is vital between us. We have one another only through Christ, but through Christ we do have one another, wholly, and for all eternity.

That dismisses once and for all every clamorous desire for something more. One who wants more than what Christ has established does not want Christian brotherhood. He is looking for some extraordinary social experience which he has not found elsewhere; he is bringing muddled and impure desires into Christian brotherhood . . .

Because God has already laid the only foundation of our fellowship, because God has bound us together in one body with other Christians in Jesus Christ, long before we entered into common life with them, we enter into that common life not as demanders but as thankful recipients. We thank God for what he has done for us. We thank God for giving us brethren who live by his call, by his forgiveness, and his promise. We do not complain of what God does not give us; we rather thank God for what he does give us daily. And is not what has been given us enough: brothers, who will go on living with us through sin and need under the blessing of his grace? Is the divine gift of Christian fellowship anything less than this, any day, even the most difficult and distressing day? Even when sin and misunderstanding burden the communal life, is not the sinning brother still a brother, with whom I, too, stand under the Word of Christ? Will not his sin be a constant occasion for me to give thanks that both of us may live in the forgiving love of God in Jesus Christ? Thus the very hour of disillusionment with my brother becomes incomparably salutary, because it so thoroughly teaches me that neither of us can ever live by our own words and deeds, but only by that one Word and Deed which really binds us together – the forgiveness of sins in Jesus Christ. When the morning mists of dreams vanish, then dawns the bright day of Christian fellowship.

In the Christian community thankfulness is just what it is anywhere else in the Christian life. Only he who gives thanks for little things receives the big things. We prevent God from giving us the great spiritual gifts he has in store for us, because we do not give thanks for daily gifts. We think we dare not be satisfied with the small measure of spiritual knowledge, experience, and love that has been given to us, and that we must constantly be looking forward eagerly for the highest good. Then we deplore the fact that we lack the deep certainty, the strong faith, and the rich experience that God has given to others, and we consider this lament to be pious. We pray for the big things and forget to give thanks for the ordinary, small (and yet really not small) gifts. How can God entrust great things to one who will not thankfully receive from him the little things? If we do not give thanks daily for the Christian fellowship in which we have been placed, even where there is no great experience, no discoverable riches, but much weakness, small faith, and difficulty; if, on the contrary, we only keep complaining to God that everything is so paltry and petty, so far from what we expected, then we hinder God from letting our fellowship grow according to the measure and riches which are there for us all in Jesus Christ.

Life Together, 7–17

Being able to let go

Because Christ stands between me and others, I dare not desire direct fellowship with them. As only Christ can speak to me in such a way that I may be saved, so others, too, can be saved only by Christ himself. This means that I must release the other person from every attempt of mine to regulate, coerce, and dominate him with my love. The other person needs to retain his independence of me; to be loved for what he is, as one for whom Christ became man, died, and rose again, for whom Christ bought forgiveness of sins and eternal life. Because Christ has long since acted decisively for my brother, before I could begin to act, I must leave him his freedom to be Christ's; I must meet him only as the person that he already is in Christ's eyes. This is the meaning of the proposition that we can meet others only through the mediation of Christ. Human love constructs its own image of the other person, of what he is and what he should become. It takes the life of the other person into its own hands. Spiritual love recognizes the true image of the other person which he has received from Jesus Christ; the image that Jesus Christ himself embodied and would stamp upon all men.

Therefore, spiritual love proves itself in that everything it says and does commends Christ. It will not seek to move others by all too personal, direct influence, by impure interference in the life of another. It will not take pleasure in pious, human fervour and excitement. It will rather meet the other person with the clear Word of God and be ready to leave him alone with this Word for a long time, willing to release him again in order that Christ may deal with him. It will respect the line that has been drawn between him and us by Christ, and it will find full fellowship with him in the Christ who alone binds us together. Thus this spiritual love will speak to Christ about a brother more than to a brother about Christ. It knows that the most direct way to others is always through prayer to Christ and that love of others is wholly dependent upon the truth in Christ.

Life Together, 22f.

Respect for the mystery of the other person

The lack of mystery in our modern life is our ruin and our poverty. The value of a human life is proportionate to the degree that it respects mystery. A human being has as much of the child in him as he respects mystery. Children have such open, watchful eyes because they know that they are surrounded by mystery. They have not yet sized up this world. They do not yet have our knowledge of how to get on with things and steer clear of mysteries. We destroy mystery because we feel that it brings us up against the boundary of our being: because we want to control everything and be lord of everything. And precisely because of that we cannot bear mystery. Mystery is alien to us because we do not feel at home in it and it speaks to us of a different home from our own.

Living without mystery means being ignorant of the mystery of our own life, of the mystery of other people, of the mystery of the world. It means passing over our own hiddenness, the hiddenness of other people and the world. It means being superficial. It means taking the world seriously only in so far as it can be calculated and exploited, not going behind the world of calculation and utility. Living without mystery means either failing to see or even denying the decisive matters of life. It means failing to see that the roots of the tree lie in the darkness of the earth, that everything that lives in the light comes from the darkness and hiddenness of a mother's womb, that all our ideas, all our spiritual life comes from the same hidden, mysterious darkness as our body, as all life. That is something that we do not want to know. We do not want to be told that mystery is the root of all that can be understood and revealed and explained. And if we are told this, we want to quantify this mystery, calculate and explain it, dissect it. And the result is that we kill life and do not discover the mystery. The mystery remains mystery. It escapes our grasp.

Now mystery does not simply mean not knowing something. The most distant star is not the greatest mystery; on the contrary, the nearer something comes to us, the better we know something, the more mysterious it becomes. It is the nearest person, not the most remote, who becomes the greatest mystery to us. And his mystery does not diminish the more we know of him. The nearer he comes, the more mysterious he becomes. The ultimate depth of the mystery is when two people come so close that they love each other. Nowhere in the world do we feel the power of mystery and its glory as strongly as here. Where two people know everything about each other, the mystery of their love becomes

21

infinitely great. And only in this love do they understand each other, are they completely aware of each other, do they completely acknowledge each other. And yet, the more they love each other and know of each other in love, the deeper they feel the mystery of their love to be. So knowledge does not do away with the mystery but deepens it. The greatest mystery is that the other is so near to me.

27 May 1934
Predigten I, 446ff.

Togetherness and solitude

Many people seek fellowship because they are afraid to be alone. Because they cannot stand loneliness, they are driven to seek the company of other people. There are Christians, too, who cannot endure being alone, who have had some bad experiences with themselves, who hope they will gain some help in association with others. They are generally disappointed. Then they blame the fellowship for what is really their own fault. The Christian community is not a spiritual sanatorium. The person who comes into a fellowship because he is running away from himself is misusing it for the sake of diversion, no matter how spiritual this diversion may appear. He is really not seeking community at all, but only distraction which will allow him to forget his loneliness for a brief time, the very alienation that creates the deadly isolation of man. The disintegration of communication and all genuine experience, and finally resignation and spiritual death are the result of such attempts to find a cure.

Let him who cannot be alone beware of community. He will only do harm to himself and to the community. Alone you stood before God when he called you; alone you had to answer that call; alone you had to struggle and pray; and alone you will die and give an account to God. You cannot escape from yourself; for God has singled you out. If you refuse to be alone you are rejecting Christ's call to you, and you can have no part in the community of those who are called. 'The challenge of death comes to us all, and no one can die for another. Everyone must fight his own battle with

22

death by himself, alone . . . I will not be with you then, nor you with me' (Luther).

But the reverse is also true: *Let him who is not in community beware of being alone.* Into the community you were called, the call was not meant for you alone; in the community of the called you bear your cross, you struggle, you pray. You are not alone, even in death, and on the Last Day you will be only one member of the great congregation of Jesus Christ. If you scorn the fellowship of the brethren, you reject the call of Jesus Christ, and thus your solitude can only be hurtful to you. 'If I die, then I am not alone in death; if I suffer they [the fellowship] suffer with me' (Luther).

We recognize, then, that only as we are within the fellowship can we be alone, and only he that is alone can live in the fellowship. Only in the fellowship do we learn to be rightly alone and only in aloneness do we learn to live rightly in the fellowship. It is not as though the one preceded the other; both begin at the same time, namely, with the call of Jesus Christ.

Each by itself has profound pitfalls and perils. One who wants fellowship without solitude plunges into the void of words and feelings, and one who seeks solitude without fellowship perishes in the abyss of vanity, self-infatuation, and despair.

Life Together, 57f.

Silence

The mark of solitude is silence, as speech is the mark of community. Silence and speech have the same inner correspondence and difference as do solitude and community. One does not exist without the other. Right speech comes out of silence, and right silence comes out of speech.

Silence does not mean dumbness, as speech does not mean chatter. Dumbness does not create solitude and chatter does not create fellowship. 'Silence is the excess, the inebriation, the victim of speech. But dumbness is unholy, like a thing only maimed, not cleanly sacrificed . . . Zacharias was speechless, instead of being silent. Had he accepted the revelation, he may perhaps have come out of the temple not dumb but silent' (Ernest Hello). The speech, the Word which establishes and binds together the fellowship, is

23

accompanied by silence. 'There is a time to keep silence and a time to speak' (Eccl. 3.7). As there are definite hours in the Christian's day for the Word, particularly the time of common worship and prayer, so the day also needs definite times of silence, silence under the Word and silence that comes out of the Word. These will be especially the times before and after hearing the Word. The Word comes not to the chatterer but to him who holds his tongue. The stillness of the temple is the sign of the holy presence of God in his Word.

There is an indifferent, or even negative, attitude towards silence which sees in it a disparagement of God's revelation in the Word. This is the view which misinterprets silence as a ceremonial gesture, as a mystical desire to get beyond the Word. This is to miss the essential relationship of silence to the Word. Silence is the simple stillness of the individual under the Word of God. We are silent before hearing the Word because our thoughts are already directed to the Word, as a child is quiet when he enters his father's room. We are silent after hearing the Word because the Word is still speaking and dwelling within us. We are silent at the beginning of the day because God should have the first word, and we are silent before going to sleep because the last word also belongs to God. We keep silence solely for the sake of the Word, and therefore not in order to show disregard for the Word but rather to honour and receive it.

Silence is nothing else but waiting for God's Word and coming from God's Word with a blessing. But everybody knows that this is something that needs to be practised and learned, in these days when talkativeness prevails. Real silence, real stillness, really holding one's tongue comes only as the sober consequence of spiritual stillness.

But this stillness before the Word will exert its influence upon the whole day. If we have learned to be silent before the Word, we shall also learn to manage our silence and our speech during the day. There is such a thing as forbidden, self-indulgent silence, a proud, offensive silence. And this means that it can never be merely silence as such. The silence of the Christian is listening silence, humble stillness, that may be interrupted at any time for the sake of humility. It is silence in conjunction with the Word. This is what Thomas à Kempis meant when he said: 'None

24

speaketh surely but he that would gladly keep silence if he might.'
There is a wonderful power of clarification, purification, and
concentration upon the essential thing in being quiet.

Life Together, 58ff.

The church and the peoples of the world

'I will hear what God the Lord will speak: for he will speak peace
unto his people, and to his saints' (Ps. 85.8). Between the twin
crags of nationalism and internationalism ecumenical
Christendom calls upon her Lord and asks his guidance.
Nationalism and internationalism have to do with political necessi-
ties and possibilities. The ecumenical church, however, does not
concern itself with these things, but with the commandments of
God, and regardless of consequences it transmits these commandments to the world.

Our task as theologians, accordingly, consists only in accepting
this commandment as a binding one, not as a question open to
discussion. Peace on earth is not a problem, but a commandment
given at Christ's coming. There are two ways of reacting to this
command from God: the unconditional, blind obedience of action,
or the hypocritical question of the Serpent: 'Yea, hath God
said . . .?' This question is the mortal enemy of obedience, and
therefore the mortal enemy of all real peace. 'Hath God not said?
Has God not understood human nature well enough to know that
wars must occur in this world, like laws of nature? Must God not
have meant that we should talk about peace, to be sure, but that
it is not to be literally translated into action? Must God not really
have said that we should work for peace, of course, but also make
ready tanks and poison gas for security?' And then perhaps the
most serious question: 'Did God say you should not protect your
own people? Did God say you should leave your own a prey to
the enemy?'

No, God did not say all that. What he has said is that there shall
be peace among men – that we shall obey him without further
question, that is what he means. He who questions the commandment of God before obeying has already denied him.

There shall be peace because of the church of Christ, for the sake of which the world exists. And this church of Christ lives at one and the same time in all peoples, yet beyond all boundaries, whether national, political, social, or racial. And the brothers who make up this church are bound together, through the commandment of the one Lord Christ, whose word they hear, more inseparably than men are bound by all the ties of common history, of blood, of class and of language. All these ties, which are part of our world, are valid ties, not indifferent; but in the presence of Christ they are not ultimate bonds. For the members of the ecumenical church, in so far as they hold to Christ, his word, his commandment of peace is more holy, more inviolable than the most revered words and works of the natural world. For they know that whoso is not able to hate father and mother for his sake is not worthy of him, and lies if he calls himself after Christ's name. These brothers in Christ obey his word; they do not doubt or question, but keep his commandment of peace. They are not ashamed, in defiance of the world, even to speak of eternal peace. They cannot take up arms against Christ himself – yet this is what they do if they take up arms against one another! Even in anguish and distress of conscience there is for them no escape from the commandment of Christ that there shall be peace.

How does peace come about? Through a system of political treaties? Through the investment of international capital in different countries? Through the big banks, through money? Or through universal peaceful rearmament in order to guarantee peace? Through none of these, for the single reason that in all of them peace is confused with safety. There is no way to peace along the way of safety. For peace must be dared. It is the great venture. It can never be safe. Peace is the opposite of security. To demand guarantees is to mistrust, and this mistrust in turn brings forth war. To look for guarantees is to want to protect oneself. Peace means to give oneself altogether to the law of God, wanting no security, but in faith and obedience laying the destiny of the nations in the hand of Almighty God, not trying to direct it for selfish purposes. Battles are won, not with weapons, but with God. They are won where the way leads to the cross. Which of us can say he knows what it might mean for the world if one nation should meet the aggressor, not with weapons in hand, but praying, defenceless, and for that very reason protected by 'a bulwark never failing'?

Once again, how will peace come? Who will call us to peace so that the world will hear, will have to hear, so that all peoples may rejoice? The individual Christian cannot do it. When all around are silent, he can indeed raise his voice and bear witness, but the powers of this world stride over him without a word. The individual church, too, can witness and suffer – oh, if it only would! – but it also is suffocated by the power of hate. Only the one great Ecumenical Council of the holy church of Christ over all the world can speak out so that the world, though it gnash its teeth, will have to hear, so that the peoples will rejoice because the church of Christ in the name of Christ has taken the weapons from the hands of their sons, forbidden war, proclaimed the peace of Christ against the raging world.

Why do we fear the fury of the world powers? Why don't we take the power from them and give it back to Christ? We can still do it today. The Ecumenical Council is in session; it can send out to all believers this radical call to peace. The nations are waiting for it in the East and in the West. Must we be put to shame by non-Christian people in the East? Shall we desert the individuals who are risking their lives for this message? The hour is late. The world is choked with weapons, and dreadful is the distrust which looks out of all men's eyes. The trumpets of war may blow tomorrow. For what are we waiting? Do we want to become involved in this guilt as never before?

> *What use to me are crown, land, folk and fame?*
> *They cannot cheer my breast.*
> *War's in the land, alas, and on my name*
> *I pray no guilt may rest (M. Claudius).*

We want to give the world a whole word, not a half word – a courageous word, a Christian word. We want to pray that this word may be given us today. Who knows if we shall see each other again another year?

No Rusty Swords, 289–92

To the natural man, the very notion of loving his enemies is an intolerable offence, and quite beyond his capacity: it cuts right across his ideas of good and evil. More important still, to man under the law, the idea of loving his enemies is clean contrary to the law of God, which requires men to sever all connection with their enemies and to pass judgment on them. Jesus however takes the law of God in his own hands and expounds its true meaning. The will of God, to which the law gives expression, is that men should defeat their enemies by loving them.

In the New Testament our enemies are those who harbour hostility against us, not those against whom we cherish hostility, for Jesus refuses to reckon with such a possibility. The Christian must treat his enemy as a brother, and requite his hostility with love. His behaviour must be determined not by the way others treat him, but by the treatment he himself receives from Jesus; it has only one source, and that is the will of Jesus.

By our enemies Jesus means those who are quite intractable and utterly unresponsive to our love, who forgive us nothing when we forgive them all, who requite our love with hatred and our service with derision, 'For the love that I had unto them, lo, they now take my contrary part: but I give myself unto prayer' (Ps. 109.4). Love asks nothing in return, but seeks those who need it. And who needs our love more than those who are consumed with hatred and are utterly devoid of love? Who in other words deserves our love more than our enemy? Where is love more glorified than where she dwells in the midst of her enemies?

Christian love draws no distinction between one enemy and another, except that the more bitter our enemy's hatred, the greater his need of love. Be his enmity political or religious, he has nothing to expect from a follower of Jesus but unqualified love. In such love there is no inner discord between private person and official capacity. In both we are disciples of Christ, or we are not Christians at all. Am I asked how this love is to behave? Jesus gives the answer: bless, do good, and pray for your enemies without reserve and without respect of persons.

'*Love your enemies.*' The preceding commandment had spoken only of the passive endurance of evil; here Jesus goes further and bids us not only to bear with evil and the evil person patiently, not only to refrain from treating him as he treats us, but actively to engage in heart-felt love towards him. We are to serve our enemy in all things without hypocrisy and with utter sincerity. No sacrifice which a lover would make for his beloved is too great for us to make for our enemy. If out of love for our brother we are willing to sacrifice goods, honour and life, we must be prepared to do the same for our enemy. We are not to imagine that this is to condone his evil; such a love proceeds from strength rather than weakness, from truth rather than fear, and therefore it cannot be guilty of the hatred of another. And who is to be the object of such a love, if not those whose hearts are stifled with hatred?

'*Bless them that persecute you.*' If our enemy cannot put up with us any longer and takes to cursing us, our immediate reaction must be to lift up our hands and bless him. Our enemies are the blessed of the Lord. Their curse can do us no harm. May their poverty be enriched with all the riches of God, with the blessing of him whom they seek to oppose in vain. We are ready to endure their curses so long as they redound to their blessing.

'*Do good to them that hate you.*' We must love not only in thought and word, but in deed, and there are opportunities of service in every circumstance of daily life. 'If thine enemy hunger, feed him; if he thirst, give him to drink' (Rom. 12.20). As brother stands by brother in distress, binding up his wounds and soothing his pain, so let us show our love towards our enemy. There is no deeper distress to be found in the world, no pain more bitter than our enemy's. Nowhere is service more necessary or more blessed than when we serve our enemies. 'It is more blessed to give than to receive.'

'*Pray for them which despitefully use you and persecute you.*' This is the supreme demand. Through the medium of prayer we go to our enemy, stand by his side, and plead for him to God. Jesus does not promise that when we bless our enemies and do good to them they will not despitefully use and persecute us. They certainly will. But not even that can hurt or overcome us so long as we pray for them. For if we pray for them, we are taking their distress and poverty, their guilt and perdition upon ourselves, and pleading to God for them. We are doing vicariously for them what they cannot do for themselves. Every insult they utter only serves to bind us more closely to God and them. Their persecution of us only serves to bring them nearer to reconciliation with God and to further the triumphs of love.

How then does love conquer? By asking not how the enemy treats her but only how Jesus treated her. The love for our enemies takes us along the way of the cross and into fellowship with the Crucified. The more we are driven along this road, the more certain is the victory of love over the enemy's hatred. For then it is not the disciple's own love, but the love of Jesus Christ alone, who for the sake of his enemies went to the cross and prayed for them as he hung there. In the face of the cross the disciples realized that they too were his enemies, and that he had overcome them by his love. It is this that opens the disciple's eyes, and enables him to see his enemy as a brother. He knows that he owes his very life to One, who though he was his enemy, treated him as a brother and accepted him, who made him his neighbour, and drew him into fellowship with himself. The disciple can now perceive that even his enemy is the object of God's love, and that he stands like himself beneath the cross of Christ. God asked us nothing about our virtues or our vices, for in his sight even our virtue was ungodliness. God's love sought out his enemies who needed it, and whom he deemed worthy of it. God loves his enemies – that is the glory of his love, as every follower of Jesus knows; through Jesus he has become a partaker in this love. For God allows his sun to shine upon the just and the unjust. But it is not only the earthly sun and the earthly rain: the 'Sun of righteousness' and the rain of God's Word which are on the sinner, and reveal the grace of the Heavenly Father. Perfect, all inclusive love is the act of the Father, it is also the act of the sons of God as it was the act of the only-begotten Son.

The Cost of Discipleship, 132–135

The polyphony of life and its many dimensions

There's always a danger in all strong, erotic love that one may love what I might call the polyphony of life. What I mean is that God wants us to love him eternally with our whole hearts – not in such a way as to injure or weaken our earthly love, but to provide a kind of *cantus firmus* to which the other melodies of life provide the counterpoint. One of these contrapuntal themes (which have their own complete independence but are yet related to the *cantus firmus*) is earthly affection. Even in the Bible we have the Song of Songs; and really one can imagine no more ardent, passionate, sensual love than is portrayed there (see 7.6). It's a good thing that the book is in the Bible, in face of all those who believe that the restraint of passion is Christian (where is there such restraint in the Old Testament?). Where the *cantus firmus* is clear and plain, the counterpoint can be developed to its limits. The two are 'undivided and yet distinct', in the words of the Chalcedonian Definition, like Christ in his divine and human natures. May not the attraction and importance of polyphony in music consist in its being a musical reflection of this christological fact and therefore of our *vita christiana*? This thought didn't occur to me till after your visit yesterday. Do you see what I'm driving at? I wanted to tell you to have a good, clear *cantus firmus*; that is the only way to a full and perfect sound, when the counterpoint has a firm support and can't come adrift or get out of tune, while remaining a distinct whole in its own right. Only a polyphony of this kind can give life a wholeness and at the same time assure us that nothing calamitous can happen as long as the *cantus firmus* is kept going. Perhaps a good deal will be easier to bear in these days together, and possibly also in the days ahead when you're separated. Please, Eberhard, do not fear and hate the separation, if it should come again with all its dangers, but rely on the *cantus firmus* – I don't know whether I've made myself clear now, but one so seldom speaks of such things . . .

I notice repeatedly here how few people there are who can harbour conflicting emotions at the same time. When bombers come, they are all fear; when there is something nice to eat, they all are greed; when they are disappointed, they are all despair; when they are successful, they can think of nothing else. They miss the fullness of life and the wholeness of an independent existence; everything objective and subjective is dissolved for them into fragments. By contrast, Christianity puts us into many different dimensions of life at the same time; we make room in ourselves, to some extent, for God and the whole world. We rejoice with those who rejoice,

31

and weep with those who weep; we are anxious (– I was again interrupted just then by the alert, and am now sitting out of doors enjoying the sun –) about our life, but at the same time we must think about things much more important to us than life itself. When the alert goes, for instance: as soon as we turn our minds from worrying about our own safety to the task of helping other people to keep calm, the situation is completely changed; life isn't pushed back into a single dimension, but is kept multi-dimensional and polyphonous. What a deliverance it is to be able to *think*, and thereby remain multi-dimensional. I've almost made it a rule here, simply to tell people who are trembling under an air raid that it would be much worse for a small town. We have to get people out of their one-track minds; that is a kind of 'preparation' for faith, or something that makes faith possible, although really it's only faith itself that can make possible a multi-dimensional life . . .

Weizsäcker's book *The World-View of Physics* is still keeping me very busy. It has again brought home to me quite clearly how wrong it is to use God as a stop-gap for the incompleteness of our knowledge. If in fact the frontiers of knowledge are being pushed further and further back (and that is bound to be the case), then God is being pushed back with them, and is therefore continually in retreat. We are to find God in what we know, not in what we don't know; God wants us to realize his presence, not in unsolved problems but in those that are solved. That is true of the relationship between God and scientific knowledge, but it is also true of the wider human problems of death, suffering, and guilt. It is now possible to find, even for these questions, human answers that take no account whatever of God. In point of fact, people deal with these questions without God (it has always been so), and it is simply not true to say that only Christianity has the answers to them. As to the idea of 'solving' problems, it may be that the Christian answers are just as unconvincing – or convincing – as any others. Here again, God is no stop-gap; he must be recognized at the centre of life, not when we are at the end of our resources; it is his will to be recognized in life, and not only when death comes; in health and vigour, and not only in suffering; in our activities, and not only in sin. The ground for this lies in the revelation of God in Jesus Christ. He is the centre of life, and he certainly didn't 'come' to answer our unsolved problems. From the centre of life certain questions, and their answers, are seen to be wholly irrelevant (I'm thinking of the judgment pronounced on Job's friends). In Christ there are no 'Christian problems'.

20 and 29 May 1944
Letters and Papers from Prison, 303, 310ff.

Fulfilled life despite unfulfilled wishes

You must be feeling particularly homesick . . . in these dangerous days, and every letter will only make it worse. But isn't it characteristic of a man, in contrast to an immature person, that his centre of gravity is always where he actually is, and that the longing for the fulfilment of his wishes cannot prevent him from being his whole self, wherever he happens to be? The adolescent is never wholly in one place; that is one of his essential characteristics, else he would presumably be a dullard. There is a wholeness about the fully grown man which enables him to face an existing situation squarely. He may have his longings, but he keeps them out of sight, and somehow masters them; and the more he has to overcome in order to live fully in the present, the more he will have the respect and confidence of his fellows, especially the younger ones, who are still on the road that he has already travelled. Desires to which we cling closely can easily prevent us from being what we ought to be and can be; and on the other hand, desires repeatedly mastered for the sake of present duty make us richer. Lack of desire is poverty. Almost all the people that I find in my present surroundings cling to their own desires, and so have no interest in others; they no longer listen, and they're incapable of loving their neighbour. I think that even in this place we ought to live as if we had no wishes and no future, and just be our true selves. It's remarkable then how others come to rely on us, confide in us, and let us talk to them. I'm writing all this to you because I think you have a big task on hand just now, and because you will be glad to think, later on, that you carried it out as well as you could. When we know that someone is in danger, we want to be sure that we know him as he really is. We can have abundant life, even though many wishes remain unfulfilled – that's what I have really been trying to say. Forgive me for putting such 'considerations' before you so persistently, but I'm sure you will understand that considering things takes up a large part of my life here. For the rest, I must add, as a necessary supplement to what I've just written, that I'm more convinced than ever that our wishes are going to be fulfilled, and that there is no need for us to throw up the sponge.

19 March 1944
Letters and Papers from Prison, 233f.

A fragment of life

The longer we are uprooted from our professional activities and our private lives, the more we feel how fragmentary our lives are, compared with those of our parents. The portraits of the great servants in Harnack's *History of the Academy* make me acutely aware of that, and almost sadden me a little. Where is there an intellectual *magnum opus* today? Where are the collecting, assimilating, and sorting of material necessary for producing such a work? Where is there today the combination of fine *abandon* and large-scale planning that goes with such a life? I doubt whether anything of the kind still exists, even among technicians and scientists, the only people who are still free to work in their own way. The end of the eighteenth century saw the end of the 'polymath', and in the nineteenth century intensive education replaced extensive, so that towards the end of it the 'specialist' evolved; and by now everyone is just a technician, even in the arts – in music the standard is high, in painting and poetry extremely moderate. This means that our cultural life remains a torso. The important thing today is that we should be able to discern from the fragment of our life how the whole was arranged and planned, and what material it consists of. For really, there are some fragments that are only worth throwing into the dustbin (even a decent 'hell' is too good for them), and others whose importance lasts for centuries, because their completion can only be a matter for God, and so they are fragments that must be fragments – I'm thinking, e.g. of the *Art of Fugue*. If our life is but the remotest reflection of such a fragment, if we accumulate, at least for a short time, a wealth of themes and weld them into a harmony in which the

34

great counterpoint is maintained from start to finish, so that at last, when it breaks off abruptly, we can sing no more than the chorale, 'I come before my throne', we will not bemoan the fragmentariness of our life, but rather rejoice in it.

23 February 1944
Letters and Papers from Prison, 219

Confidence in one's own work

I haven't yet answered your remarks about Michelangelo, Burckhardt, and *hilaritas*. I found them illuminating – at any rate, what you say about Burckhardt's theses. But surely *hilaritas* means not only serenity, in the classical sense of the word (Raphael and Mozart); Walther v.d. Vogelweide, the Knight of Bamberg, Luther, Lessing, Rubens, Hugo Wolf, Karl Barth – to mention only a few – also have a kind of *hilaritas*, which I might describe as confidence in their own work, boldness and defiance of the world and of popular opinion, a steadfast certainty that in their own work they are showing the world something *good* (even if the world doesn't like it), and a high-spirited self-confidence. I admit that Michelangelo, Rembrandt and, at a considerable remove, Kierkegaard and Nietzsche, are in quite a different category from those that I've mentioned. There is something less assertive, evident, and final in their works, less conviction, detachment, and humour. All the same, I think some of them are characterized by *hilaritas* in the sense that I've described, as a necessary attribute of greatness. Here is Burckhardt's limitation, probably a conscious one.

I've recently been studying the mature 'worldliness' of the thirteenth century, conditioned, not by the Renaissance, but by the Middle Ages, and presumably by the struggle between the *idea of the emperor* and the papacy. (Walther, the Nibelungen, Parsifal – what surprising tolerance of the Mohammedans in the figure of Parsifal's half-brother Feirefiz! – Naumburg and Magdeburgh cathedrals.) This worldliness is not 'emancipated', but 'Christian', even if it is anti-clerical. Where did this 'worldliness', so essentially different from that of the Renaissance, stop? A trace of it seems to survive in Lessing – in contrast to the Western Enlightenment – and in a different way in Goethe, then later in

Stifter and Mörike (to say nothing of Claudius and Gotthelf), but nowhere in Schiller and the Idealists. It would be very useful to draw up a good genealogy here.

9 March 1944
Letters and Papers from Prison, 229f.

Friendship

I very much agree with what you say in this connection about friendship which, in contrast to marriage and kinship, has no generally recognized rights, and therefore depends entirely on its own inherent quality. It is by no means easy to classify friendship sociologically. Perhaps it is to be regarded as a sub-heading of culture and education, brotherhood being a sub-heading of church, and comradeship a sub-heading of work and politics. Marriage, work, state, and church all have their definite, divine mandate; but what about culture and education? I don't think they can just be classified under work, however tempting that might be in many ways.

They belong, not to the sphere of obedience, but to the broad area of freedom, which surrounds all three spheres of the divine mandates. The man who is ignorant of this area of freedom may be a good father, citizen, and worker, indeed even a Christian; but I doubt whether he is a complete man and therefore a Christian in the widest sense of the term. Our 'Protestant' (not Lutheran) Prussian world has been so dominated by the four mandates that the sphere of freedom has receded into the background. I wonder whether it is possible (it almost seems so today) to regain the idea of the church as providing an understanding of the area of freedom (art, education, friendship, play), so that Kierkegaard's 'aesthetic existence' would not be banished from the church's sphere, but would be re-established within it? I really think that is so, and it would mean that we should recover a link with the Middle Ages. Who is there, for instance, in our times, who can devote himself with an easy mind to music, friendship, games, or happiness? Surely not the 'ethical' man, but only the Christian. Just because friendship belongs to this sphere of freedom ('of the Christian man'?!), it must be confidently defended against all the disapproving frowns of 'ethical' existence, though without claiming for it the *necessitas* of a divine decree, but only the *necessitas* of *freedom*. I believe that within the sphere of this freedom friendship is by far the rarest and most priceless treasure, for where else does it survive in this world of ours, dominated as it is by the *three other* mandates? It cannot be compared with the treasures of the mandates, for in relation to them it is *sui generis*; it belongs to them as the cornflower belongs to the cornfield.

23 January 1944
Letters and Papers from Prison, 192f.

Who is Christ for us today?

What is bothering me incessantly is the question what Christianity really is, or indeed who Christ really is, for us today. The time when people could be told everything by means of words, whether theological or pious, is over, and so is the time of inwardness and conscience – and that means the time of religion in general. We are moving towards a completely religionless time; people as they are now simply cannot be religious any more. Even those who honestly describe themselves as 'religious' do not in the least act up to it, and so they presumably mean something quite different by 'religious'.

Our whole nineteen-hundred-year-old Christian preaching and theology rest on the 'religious *a priori*' of mankind. 'Christianity' has always been a form – perhaps the true form – of 'religion'. But if one day it becomes clear that this *a priori* does not exist at all, but was a historically conditioned and transient form of human self-expression, and if therefore man becomes radically religion-less – and I think that that is already more or less the case (else how is it, for example, that this war, in contrast to all previous ones, is not calling forth any 'religious' reaction?) – what does that mean for 'Christianity'? It means that the foundation is taken away from the whole of what has up to now been our 'Christianity', and that there remain only a few 'last survivors of the age of chivalry', or a few intellectually dishonest people, on whom we can descend as 'religious'. Are they to be the chosen few? Is it on this dubious group of people that we are to pounce in fervour, pique, or indignation, in order to sell them our goods? Are we to fall upon a few unfortunate people in their hour of need and exercise a sort of religious compulsion on them? If we don't want to do all that, if our final judgment must be that the western form of Christianity, too, was only a preliminary stage to a complete absence of religion, what kind of situation emerges for us, for the church? How can Christ become the Lord of the religionless as well? Are there religionless Christians? If religion is only a garment of Christianity – and even this garment has looked very different at different times – then what is a religionless Christianity?

Barth, who is the only one to have started along this line of thought, did not carry it to completion, but arrived at a positivism of revelation, which in the last analysis is essentially a restoration. For the religionless working man (or any other man) nothing decisive is gained here. The questions to be answered would surely be: What do a church, a community, a sermon, a liturgy, a Christian life mean in a religionless world? How do we speak of God – without religion, i.e. without the temporally conditioned presuppositions of metaphysics, inwardness, and so on? How do we speak (or perhaps we cannot now even 'speak' as we used to) in a 'secular' way about 'God'? In what way are we 'religionless-secular' Christians, in what way are we the ἐκ-κλησία, those who are called forth, not regarding ourselves from a religious point of view as specially favoured, but rather as belonging wholly to the world? In that case Christ is no longer an object of religion, but something quite different, really the Lord of the world. But what does that mean? What is the place of worship and prayer in a religionless situation? Does the secret discipline, or alternatively the difference (which I have suggested to you before) between penultimate and ultimate, take on a new importance here? . . .

I often ask myself why a 'Christian instinct' often draws me more to the religionless people than to the religious, by which I don't in the least mean with any evangelizing intention, but, I might almost say, 'in brotherhood'. While I'm often reluctant to mention God by name to religious people – because that name somehow seems to me here not to ring true, and I feel myself to be slightly dishonest (it's particularly bad when others start to talk in religious jargon; I then dry up almost completely and feel awkward and uncomfortable) – to people with no religion I can on occasion mention him by name quite calmly and as a matter of course. Religious people speak of God when human knowledge (perhaps simply because they are too lazy to think) has come to an end, or when human resources fail – in fact it is always the *deus ex machina* that they bring on to the scene, either for the apparent solution of insoluble problems, or as strength in human failure – always, that is to say, exploiting human weakness or human boundaries. Of necessity, that can go on only till people can by their own strength push these boundaries somewhat further out, so that God becomes superfluous as a *deus ex machina*. I've come to be doubtful of talking about any human boundaries (is even death, which people now hardly fear, and is sin, which they now hardly understand, still a genuine boundary today?). It always seems to me that we are trying anxiously in this way to reserve some space for God; I should like to speak of God not on the boundaries but at the centre, not in weaknesses but in strength; and therefore not in death and guilt but in man's life and goodness. As to the boundaries, it seems to me better to be silent and leave the insoluble unsolved. Belief in the resurrection is *not* the 'solution' of the problem of death. God's 'beyond' is not the beyond of our cognitive faculties. The transcendence of epistemological theory has nothing to do with the transcendence of God. God is beyond in the midst of our life. The church stands, not at the boundaries where human powers give out, but in the middle of the village. That is how it is in the Old Testament, and in this sense we still read the New Testament far too little in the light of the Old. How this religionless Christianity looks, what form it takes, is something that I'm thinking about a great deal, and I shall be writing to you again about it soon. It may be that on us in particular, midway between East and West, there will fall a heavy responsibility.

30 April 1944
Letters and Papers from Prison, 279–282

Renewal of the world

What does it mean to 'interpret in a religious sense'? I think it means to speak on the one hand metaphysically, and on the other hand individualistically. Neither of these is relevant to the biblical message or to the man of today. Hasn't the individualistic question about personal salvation almost completely left us all? Aren't we really under the impression that there are more important things than that question (perhaps not more important than the *matter* itself, but more important than the *question*!)? I know it sounds pretty monstrous to say that. But, fundamentally, isn't this in fact biblical? Does the question about saving one's soul appear in the Old Testament at all? Aren't righteousness and the Kingdom of God on earth the focus of everything, and isn't it true that Rom. 3.24ff, is not an individualistic doctrine of salvation, but the culmination of the view that God alone is righteous? It is not with the beyond that we are concerned, but with this world as created and preserved, subjected to laws, reconciled, and restored. What is above this world is, in the gospel, intended to exist *for* this world; I mean that, not in the anthropocentric sense of liberal, mystic pietistic, ethical theology, but in the biblical sense of the creation and of the incarnation, crucifixion, and resurrection of Jesus Christ.

5 May 1944
Letters and Papers from Prison, 285f.

Recollection transformed in peace

I should like to say something to help you in the time of separation that lies ahead. There is no need to say how hard any such separation is for us; but as I've now been separated for nine months from all the people that I'm devoted to, I should like to pass on to you something of what I have learnt . . .

First: nothing can make up for the absence of someone whom we love, and it would be wrong to try to find a substitute; we must simply hold out and see it through. That sounds very hard at first, but at the same time it is a great consolation, for the gap, as long as it remains unfilled, preserves the bonds between us. It is nonsense to say that God fills the gap; he doesn't fill it, but on the contrary, he keeps it empty and so helps us to keep alive our former communion with each other, even at the cost of pain.

Secondly: the dearer and richer our memories, the more difficult the separation. But gratitude changes the pangs of memory into a tranquil joy. The beauties of the past are borne, not as a thorn in the flesh, but as a precious gift in themselves. We must take care not to wallow in our memories or hand ourselves over to them, just as we do not gaze all the time at a valuable present, but only at special times, and apart from these keep it, simply as a hidden treasure that is ours for certain. In this way the past gives us lasting joy and strength.

Thirdly: times of separation are not a total loss or unprofitable for our companionship, or at any rate they need not be so. In spite of all the difficulties that they bring, they can be the means of strengthening fellowship quite remarkably.

Fourthly: I've learnt here especially that the *facts* can always be mastered, and that difficulties are magnified out of all proportion simply by fear and anxiety. From the moment we wake until we fall asleep we must commend other people wholly and unreservedly to God and leave them in his hands, and transform our anxiety for them into prayers on their behalf:

> With sorrow and with grief . . .
> God *will not* be distracted.
> > 24 December 1943
> > *Letters and Papers from Prison*, 176f.

II · ACTION

Introduction

'We have spent too much time in thinking, supposing that if we weigh in advance the possibilities of any action, it will happen automatically. We have learnt, rather too late, that action comes, not from thought, but from a readiness for responsibility' (*Letters and Papers from Prison*, 298). The sentences mark a major turning point in Bonhoeffer's life. They are an acknowledgment of weakness, if not of guilt. At all events they are a repudiation of the past, of the ways of thinking and acting which had gone before, not only in Bonhoeffer's own generation but over whole generations of the leading intellectual circles in Germany. Bonhoeffer explicitly includes himself in the failure of these ways. People were accustomed to find their place in already existing forms and orders of life. It was in that context that they sought to make their contribution. Responsibily was limited to tasks within this order. That was true even more, and to an intensified degree, in the church's understanding of itself. There was no consciousness of any mandate for the whole, any responsibility for the form that public, state life should take.

The change in Bonhoeffer's own life necessarily followed when all power and responsibility for its use fell into the hands of people who were themselves beyond all responsibility. There was virtually no precedent for what ways should now be taken, what decisions should now be made, what acts should now be performed. The way led through unknown and dangerous territory. Only a few Christians dared to tread this pioneering course in Germany and to affirm it in such unqualified terms as did Bonhoeffer in his thought and action. His thinking is never a later justification for his action, but a presupposition of it. Yet on the other hand it is arrived at only through action. Bonhoeffer's fragments on ethics provide documentation for this twofold point of reference. Anyone who reads the fragments will feel drawn into the problems of existence at that time (and is it only that time? is it not also our own?), in the process being led to make a more appropriate response. This cannot be done without a recasting of current ideas, always surprising, sometimes painful, but ultimately always liberating and encouraging, as we find in the section on 'What is meant by "telling the truth"?' or the chapter on the conscience.

The central content of the second section of this book is the essay 'After Ten Years'. All the other contributions are grouped around it. Bonhoeffer wrote it at the end of 1942, a few months before his arrest, and gave it to some of his closest friends and allies in the cause, as an incorruptible account of how things were, as an acute analysis of the present, as a compendium of truths to be kept in view no matter what happened, and at least as an assurance of the way that had to be followed. What could not be provided in the few pages of this document, and indeed did not have to be provided, can be read in the sections on 'representation', 'taking over guilt' and 'the conscience' (all from *Ethics*): namely, how everything that is said here is exclusively and adequately rooted in a bond with Jesus Christ. We do not understand Bonhoeffer at all unless we see that his political course is an act of following Christ, a special form of discipleship, but one which was inevitable for him. And for us, for our churches, and for world Christianity, that is a real blessing.

O.D.

Only those who are obedient believe

Discipleship means adherence to Christ, and, because Christ is the object of that adherence, it must take the form of discipleship. An abstract christology, a doctrinal system, a general religious knowledge on the subject of grace or on the forgiveness of sins, render discipleship superfluous, and in fact they positively exclude any idea of discipleship whatever, and are essentially

43

inimical to the whole conception of following Christ. With an abstract idea it is possible to enter into a relation of formal knowledge, to become enthusiastic about it, and perhaps even to put it into practice; but it can never be followed in personal obedience. Christianity without the living Christ is inevitably Christianity without discipleship, and Christianity without discipleship is always Christianity without Christ. It remains an abstract idea, a myth which has a place for the Fatherhood of God, but omits Christ as the living Son. And a Christianity of that kind is nothing more nor less than the end of discipleship. In such a religion there is trust in God, but no following of Christ. Because the Son of God became Man, because he is the Mediator, for that reason alone the only true relation we can have with him is to follow him. Discipleship is bound to Christ as the Mediator, and where it is properly understood, it necessarily implies faith in the Son of God as the Mediator. Only the Mediator, the God-Man, can call men to follow him.

Discipleship without Jesus Christ is a way of our own choosing. It may be the ideal way. It may even lead to martyrdom, but it is devoid of all promise. Jesus will certainly reject it.

The idea of a situation in which faith is possible is only a way of stating the facts of a case in which the following two propositions hold good and are equally true: *only he who believes is obedient, and only he who is obedient believes.*

It is quite unbiblical to hold the first proposition without the second. We think we understand when we hear that obedience is possible only where there is faith. Does not obedience follow faith as good fruit grows on a good tree? First, faith, then obedience. If by that we mean that it is faith which justifies, and not the act of obedience, all well and good, for that is the essential and unexceptionable presupposition of all that follows. If, however, we make a chronological distinction between faith and obedience, and make obedience subsequent to faith, we are divorcing the one from the other – and then we get the practical question, when must obedience begin? Obedience remains separated from faith. From the point of view of justification it is necessary thus to separate them, but we must never lose sight of their essential unity. For faith is only real when there is obedience, never without it, and faith only becomes faith in the act of obedience.

Since, then, we cannot adequately speak of obedience as the consequence of faith, and since we must never forget the indissoluble unity of the two, we must place the one proposition that only he who believes is obedient alongside the other, that only he who is obedient believes. In the one case faith is the condition of obedience, and in the other obedience the condition of faith. In exactly the same way in which obedience is called the consequence of faith, it must also be called the presupposition of faith.

Only the obedient believe. If we are to believe, we must obey a concrete command. Without this preliminary step of obedience, our faith will only be pious humbug, and lead us to the grace which is not costly.

The Cost of Discipleship, 50, 54f.

New tasks

My recent activity, which has been very much in the secular sphere, keeps giving me a good deal to think about. I am amazed that for days I live, and can live, without the Bible. I would not find it obedience but auto-suggestion if I were to force myself to read the Bible. I know that such auto-suggestion could be, and is, a great help, but I am afraid that it might falsify a real experience and ultimately not prove to be a real help. Then when I open the Bible again, I find it new and satisfying as never before, and I would love to preach again. I know that I need only open my own books to hear all the arguments against this. I don't want to justify myself, but I recognize that in spiritual terms I have had much richer times. Nevertheless, I can feel how resistance against all that is religious is growing in me, often to the point of an instinctive abhorrence – and that is surely not a good thing. I am not religious by nature. But I must constantly think of God and of Christ, and authenticity, life, freedom and mercy are still very important to me. But in religious garb they are so unattractive. Do you understand? All these are by no means new thoughts and insights, but since I believe that knots are being untied for me here, I'm letting things run their course and not opposing them. That is also

45

the way in which I am understanding my activity in the secular sector. Please excuse these confessions; blame them on the long railway journey. We must find time to talk again about these things in peace.

25 June 1942
Gesammelte Schriften II, 420f.

Christ and good people

'Blessed are they which are persecuted for righteousness' sake: for theirs is the kingdom of heaven' (Matt. 5.10). This does not refer to the righteousness of God; it does not refer to persecution for Jesus Christ's sake. It is the beatification of those who are persecuted for the sake of a just cause, and, as we may now add, for the sake of a true, good and human cause (*cf.* I Peter 3.14 and 2.20). This beatitude puts those Christians entirely in the wrong who, in their mistaken anxiety to act rightly, seek to avoid any suffering for the sake of a just, good and true cause, because, as they maintain, they could with a clear conscience suffer only for an explicit profession of faith in Christ; it rebukes them for their ungenerousness and narrowness which looks with suspicion on all suffering for a just cause and keeps its distance from it. Jesus gives his support to those who suffer for the sake of a just cause, even if this cause is not precisely the confession of his name; he takes them under his protection, he accepts responsibility for them, and he lays claim to them. And so the man who is persecuted for the sake of a just cause is led to Christ, so that it happens that in the hour of suffering and of responsibility, perhaps for the first time in his life and in a way which is strange and surprising to him but is nevertheless an inner necessity, such a man appeals to Christ and professes himself a Christian because at this moment, for the first time, he becomes aware that he belongs to Christ. This, too, is not an abstract deduction, but it is an experience which we ourselves have undergone, an experience in which the power of Jesus Christ became manifest in fields of life where it had previously remained unknown.

In times of established order, when the law rules supreme and the transgressor of the law is disgraced and ostracized, it is in relation to the tax-gatherer and the prostitute that the gospel of Jesus Christ discloses itself most clearly to men. 'The publicans and the harlots go into the kingdom of heaven before you' (Matt. 21.31). In times which are out of joint, in times when lawlessness and wickedness triumph in complete unrestraint, it is rather in relation to the few remaining just, truthful and human men that the gospel will make itself known. It was the experience of other times that the wicked found their way to Christ while the good remained remote from him. The experience of our own time is that it is the good who find their way back to Christ and that the wicked obstinately remain aloof from him. Other times could preach that a man must first become a sinner, like the publican and the harlot, before he could know and find Christ, but we in our time must say rather that before a man can know and find Christ he must first become righteous like those who strive and who suffer for the sake of justice, truth and humanity. Both of these principles are alike paradoxical and in themselves impossible; but they make the situation clear. Christ belongs both to the wicked and to the good; he belongs to them both only as sinners, that is to say, as men who in their wickedness and in their goodness have fallen away from the origin. He summons them back to the origin so that they shall no longer be good and evil but justified and sanctified sinners. But before we express this ultimate in which evil and good are one before Christ and in which the difference between all times is annulled before Christ, we must not avoid the question which is set us by our own experience and by our own time, the question of what is meant by saying that the good find Christ, in other words the question of the relationship of Jesus Christ to good people and to goodness.

Ethics, 42ff.

After ten years

Ten years is a long time in anyone's life. As time is the most valuable thing that we have, because it is the most irrevocable, the thought of any lost time troubles us whenever we look back. Time lost is time in which we have failed to live a full human life, gain experience, learn, create, enjoy, and suffer; it is time that has not

been filled up, but left empty. These last years have certainly not
been like that. Our losses have been great and immeasurable, but
time has not been lost. It is true that the knowledge and experience
that were gained, and of which one did not become conscious till
later, are only abstractions of reality, of life actually lived. But just
as the capacity to forget is a gift of grace, so memory, the recalling
of lessons we have learnt, is also part of responsible living. In the
following pages I should like to try to give some account of what
we have experienced and learnt in common during these years –
not personal experiences, or anything systematically arranged, or
arguments and theories, but conclusions reached more or less in
common by a circle of like-minded people, and related to the
business of human life, put down one after the other, the only
connection between them being that of concrete experience. There
is nothing new about them, for they were known long before; but
it has been given to us to reach them anew by first-hand experience.
One cannot write about these things without a constant sense of
gratitude for the fellowship of spirit and community of life that
have been proved and preserved thoughout these years.

No ground under our feet

One may ask whether there have ever before in human history
been people with so little ground under their feet – people to
whom every available alternative seemed equally intolerable,
repugnant, and futile, who looked beyond all these existing
alternatives for the source of their strength so entirely in the past
or in the future, and who yet, without being dreamers, were able
to await the success of their cause so quietly and confidently. Or
perhaps one should rather ask whether the responsible thinking
people of any generation that stood at a turning-point in history
did not feel much as we do, simply because something new was
emerging that could not be seen in the existing alternatives.

Who stands fast?

The great masquerade of evil has played havoc with all our ethical
concepts. For evil to appear disguised as light, charity, historical
necessity, or social justice is quite bewildering to anyone brought
up on our traditional ethical concepts, while for the Christian who

bases his life on the Bible it merely confirms the fundamental wickedness of evil.

The 'reasonable' people's failure is obvious. With the best intentions and a naïve lack of realism, they think that with a little reason they can bend back into position the framework that has got out of joint. In their lack of vision they want to do justice to all sides, and so the conflicting forces wear them down with nothing achieved. Disappointed by the world's unreasonableness, they see themselves condemned to ineffectiveness; they step aside in resignation or collapse before the stronger party.

Still more pathetic is the total collapse of moral *fanaticism*. The fanatic thinks that his single-minded principles qualify him to do battle with the powers of evil; but like a bull he rushes at the red cloak instead of the person who is holding it; he exhausts himself and is beaten. He gets entangled in non-essentials and falls into the trap set by cleverer people.

Then there is the man with a *conscience*, who fights single-handed against heavy odds in situations that call for a decision. But the scale of the conflicts in which he has to choose – with no advice or support except from his own conscience – tears him to pieces. Evil approaches him in so many respectable and seductive disguises that his conscience becomes nervous and vacillating, till at last he contents himself with a salved instead of a clear conscience, so that he lies to his own conscience in order to avoid despair; for a man whose only support is his conscience can never realize that a bad conscience may be stronger and more wholesome than a deluded one.

From the perplexingly large number of possible decisions, the way of *duty* seems to be the sure way out. Here, what is commanded is accepted as what is most certain, and the responsibility for it rests on the commander, not on the person commanded. But no one who confines himself to the limits of duty ever goes so far as to venture, on his sole responsibility, to act in the only way that makes it possible to score a direct hit on evil and defeat it. The man of duty will in the end have to do his duty by the devil too.

As to the man who asserts his complete *freedom* to stand four-square to the world, who values the necessary deed more highly than an unspoilt conscience or reputation, who is ready to sacrifice a barren principle for a fruitful compromise, or the barren wisdom of a middle course for a fruitful radicalism – let him beware lest his freedom should bring him down. He will assent to what is bad so as to ward off something worse, and in doing so he will no longer be able to realize that the worse, which he wants to avoid, might be the better. Here we have the raw material of tragedy.

Here and there people flee from public altercation into the sanctuary of private *virtuousness*. But anyone who does this must shut his mouth and his eyes to the injustice around him. Only at the cost of self-deception can he keep himself pure from the contamination arising from responsible action. In spite of all that he does, what he leaves undone will rob him of his peace of mind. He will either go to pieces because of this disquiet, or become the most hypocritcal of Pharisees.

Who stands fast? Only the man whose final standard is not his reason, his principles, his conscience, his freedom, or his virtue, but who is ready to sacrifice all this when he is called to obedient and responsible action in faith and in exclusive allegiance to God – the responsible man, who tries to make his whole life an answer to the question and call of God. Where are these responsible people?

Civil courage?

What lies behind the complaint about the dearth of civil courage? In recent years we have seen a great deal of bravery and self-sacrifice, but civil courage hardly anywhere, even among ourselves. To attribute this simply to personal cowardice would be too facile a psychology; its background is quite different. In a long history, we Germans have had to learn the need for and the strength of obedience. In the subordination of all personal wishes and ideas to the tasks to which we have been called, we have seen the meaning and the greatness of our lives. We have looked upwards, not in servile fear, but in free trust, seeing in our tasks a call, and in our call a vocation. This readiness to follow a command from 'above' rather than our own private opinions and wishes was a sign of legitimate self-distrust. Who would deny that in obedience, in their task and calling, the Germans have again and again shown the utmost bravery and self-sacrifice? But the German has kept his freedom – and what nation has talked more passionately of freedom than the Germans, from Luther to the idealist philosophers? – by seeking deliverance from self-will through service to the community. Calling and freedom were to him two sides of the same thing. But in this he misjudged the world; he did not realize that his submissiveness and self-sacrifice could be exploited for evil ends. When that happened, the exercise of the calling itself became questionable, and all the moral principles of the German were bound to totter. The fact could not be escaped that the German still lacked something fundamental: he could not see the need for free and responsible action, even in opposition to his task and his calling; in its place there appeared on the one hand an irresponsible lack of scruple, and on the other a self-tormenting punctiliousness that never led to action. Civil courage, in fact, can grow only out of the free responsibility of free men. Only now are the Germans beginning to discover the meaning of free responsibility. It depends on a God who demands responsible action in a bold venture of faith, and who promises forgiveness and consolation to the man who becomes a sinner in that venture.

Of success

Although it is certainly not true that success justifies an evil deed and shady means, it is impossible to regard success as something that is ethically quite neutral. The fact is that historical success creates a basis for the continuance of life, and it is still a moot point whether it is ethically more responsible to take the field like a Don Quixote against a new age, or to admit one's defeat, accept the new age, and agree to serve it. In the last resort success makes history; and the ruler of history repeatedly brings good out of evil over the heads of the history-makers. Simply to ignore the ethical significance of success is a short-circuit created by dogmatists who think unhistorically and irresponsibly; and it is good for us sometimes to be compelled to grapple seriously with the ethical problem of success. As long as goodness is successful, we can afford the luxury of regarding it as having no ethical significance; it is when success is achieved by evil means that the problem arises. In the face of such a situation we find that it cannot be adequately dealt with, either by theoretical dogmatic arm-chair criticism, which means a refusal to face the facts, or by opportunism, which means giving up the struggle and surrendering to success. We will not and must not be either outraged critics or opportunists, but must take our share of responsibility for the moulding of history in every situation and at every moment, whether we are the victors or the vanquished. One who will not allow any occurrence whatever to deprive him of his responsibility for the course of history – because he knows that it has been laid on him by God – will thereafter achieve a more fruitful relation to the events of history than that of barren criticism and equally barren opportunism. To talk of going down fighting like heroes in the face of certain defeat is not really heroic at all, but merely a refusal to face the future. The ultimate question for a responsible man to ask is not how he is to extricate himself heroically from the affair, but how the coming generation is to live. It is only from this question, with its responsibility towards history, that fruitful solutions can come, even if for the time being they are very humiliating. In short, it is much easier to see a thing through from the point of view of abstract principle than from that of concrete responsibility. The rising generation will always instinctively discern which of these we make the basis of our actions, for it is their own future that is at stake.

Of folly

Folly is a more dangerous enemy to the good than evil. One can protest against evil; it can be unmasked and, if need be, prevented by force. Evil always carries the seeds of its own destruction, as it makes people, at the least, uncomfortable. Against folly we have no defence. Neither protests nor force can touch it; reasoning is no use; facts that contradict personal prejudices can simply be disbelieved – indeed, the fool can counter by criticizing them, and if they are undeniable, they can just be pushed aside as trivial exceptions. So the fool, as distinct from the scoundrel, is completely self-satisfied; in fact, he can easily become dangerous, as it does not take much to make him aggressive. A fool must therefore be treated more cautiously than a scoundrel; we shall never again try to convince a fool by reason, for it is both useless and dangerous.

If we are to deal adequately with folly, we must try to understand its nature. This much is certain, that it is a moral rather than an intellectual defect. There are people who are mentally agile but foolish, and people who are mentally slow but very far from foolish – a discovery that we make to our surprise as a result of particular situations. We thus get the impression that folly is likely to be, not a congenital defect, but one that is acquired in certain circumstances where people *make* fools of themselves or allow others to make fools of them. We notice further that this defect is less common in the unsociable and solitary than in individuals or groups that are inclined or condemned to sociability. It seems, then, that folly is a sociological rather than a psychological problem, and that it is a special form of the operation of historical circumstances on people, a psychological by-product of definite external factors. If we look more closely, we see that any violent display of power, whether political or religious, produces an outburst of folly in a large part of mankind; indeed, this seems actually to be a psychological and sociological law: the power of some needs the folly of the others. It is not that certain human capacities, intellectual capacities for instance, become stunted or destroyed, but rather that the upsurge of power makes such an overwhelming impression that men are deprived of their independent judgment, and – more or less unconsciously – give up trying to assess the new state of affairs for themselves. The fact that the fool is often stubborn must not mislead us into thinking that he is independent. One feels in fact, when talking to him, that one is dealing, not with the man himself, but with slogans, catchwords, and the like, which have taken hold of him. He is under a spell, he is blinded, his very nature is being misused and exploited. Having thus become a passive instrument, the fool will be capable of any evil and at the same time incapable of seeing that it is evil. Here lies the danger of a diabolical exploitation that can do irreparable damage to human beings.

But at this point it is quite clear, too, that folly can be overcome, not by instruction, but only by an act of liberation; and so we have come to terms with the fact that in the great majority of cases inward liberation must be preceded by outward liberation, and that until that has taken place, we may as well abandon all attempts to convince the fool. In this state of affairs we have to realize why it is no use our trying to find out what 'the people' really think, and why the question is so superfluous for the man who thinks and acts responsibly – but always given these particular circumstances.

The Bible's words that 'the fear of the Lord is the beginning of wisdom' (Ps. 111.10) tell us that a person's inward liberation to live a responsible life before God is the only real cure for folly.

But there is some consolation in these thoughts on folly: they in no way justify us in thinking that most people are fools in all circumstances. What will really matter is whether those in power expect more from people's folly than from their wisdom and independence of mind.

Contempt for humanity?

There is a very real danger of our drifting into an attitude of contempt for humanity. We know quite well that we have no right to do so, and that it would lead us into the most sterile relation to our fellow-men. The following thoughts may keep us from such a temptation. It means that we at once fall into the worst blunders of our opponents. The man who despises another will never be able to make anything of him. Nothing that we despise in the other man is entirely absent from ourselves. We often expect from others more than we are willing to do ourselves. Why have we hitherto thought so intemperately about man and his frailty and temptability? We must learn to regard people less in the light of what they do or omit to do, and more in the light of what they suffer. The only profitable relationship to others – and especially to our weaker brethren – is one of love, and that means the will to hold fellowship with them. God himself did not despise humanity, but became man for men's sake.

Immanent righteousness

It is one of the most surprising experiences, but at the same time one of the most incontrovertible, that evil – often in a surprisingly short time – proves its own folly and defeats its own object. That does not mean that punishment follows hard on the heels of every evil action; but it does mean that deliberate transgression of the divine law in the supposed interests of worldly self-preservation has exactly the opposite effect. We learn this from our own experience, and we can interpret it in various ways. At least it seems possible to infer with certainty that in social life there are laws more powerful than anything that may claim to dominate them, and that it is therefore not only wrong but unwise to disregard them. We can understand from this why Aristotelian-Thomist ethics made wisdom one of the cardinal virtues. Wisdom and folly are not ethically indifferent, as Neo-protestant motive-ethics would have it. In the fullness of the concrete situation and the possibilities which it offers, the wise man at the same time recognizes the impassable limits that are set to all action by the permanent laws of human social life; and in this knowledge the wise man acts well and the good man wisely.

It is true that all historically important action is constantly overstepping the limits set by these laws. But it makes all the difference whether such overstepping of the appointed limits is regarded in principle as the superseding of them, and is therefore given out to be a law of a special kind, or whether the overstepping is deliberately regarded as a fault which is perhaps unavoidable, justified only if the law and the limit are re-established and respected as soon as possible. It is not necessarily hypocrisy if the declared aim of political action is the restoration of the law, and not mere self-preservation. The world *is*, in fact, so ordered that a basic respect for ultimate laws and human life is also the best means of self-preservation, and that these laws may be broken only on the odd occasion in case of brief necessity, whereas anyone who turns necessity into a principle, and in so doing establishes a law of his own alongside them, is inevitably bound, sooner or later, to suffer retribution. The immanent righteousness of history rewards and punishes only men's deeds, but the eternal righteousness of God tries and judges their hearts.

A few articles of faith on the sovereignty of God in history

I believe that God can and will bring good out of evil, even out of the greatest evil. For that purpose he needs men who make the best use of everything. I believe that God will give us all the strength we need to help us to resist in all time of distress. But he never gives it in advance, lest we should rely on ourselves and not on him alone. A faith such as this should allay all our fears for the future. I believe that even our mistakes and shortcomings are turned to good account, and that it is no harder for God to deal with them than with our supposedly good deeds. I believe that God is no timeless fate, but that he waits for and answers sincere prayers and responsible actions.

55

Confidence

There is hardly one of us who has not known what it is to be betrayed. The figure of Judas, which we used to find so difficult to understand, is now fairly familiar to us. The air that we breathe is so polluted by mistrust that it almost chokes us. But where we have broken through the layer of mistrust, we have been able to discover a confidence hitherto undreamed of. Where we trust, we have learnt to put our very lives into the hands of others; in the face of all the different interpretations that have been put on our lives and actions, we have learnt to trust unreservedly. We now know that only such confidence, which is always a venture, though a glad and positive venture, enables us really to live and work. We know that it is most reprehensible to sow and encourage mistrust, and that our duty is rather to foster and strengthen confidence wherever we can. Trust will always be one of the greatest, rarest, and happiest blessings of our life in community, though it can emerge only on the dark background of a necessary mistrust. We have learnt never to trust a scoundrel an inch, but to give ourselves to the trustworthy without reserve.

The sense of quality

Unless we have the courage to fight for a revival of wholesome reserve between man and man, we shall perish in an anarchy of human values. The impudent contempt for such reserve is the mark of the rabble, just as inward uncertainty, haggling and cringing for the favour of insolent people, and lowering oneself to the level of the rabble are the way of becoming no better than the rabble oneself. When we forget what is due to ourselves and to others, when the feeling for human quality and the power to exercise reserve cease to exist, chaos is at the door. When we tolerate impudence for the sake of material comforts, then we abandon our self-respect, the flood-gates are opened, chaos bursts the dam that we were to defend; and we are responsible for it all. In other times it may have been the business of Christianity to champion the equality of all men; its business today will be to defend passionately human dignity and reserve. The misinterpretation that we are acting for our own interests, and the cheap insinuation that our attitude is anti-social, we shall simply have to put up with; they are the invariable protests of the rabble against decency and order. Anyone who is pliant and uncertain in this matter does not realize what is at stake, and indeed in his case the reproaches may well be justified. We are witnessing the levelling down of all ranks of society, and at the same time the birth of a new sense of nobility, which is binding together a circle of men from all former social classes. Nobility arises from and exists by sacrifice, courage, and a clear sense of duty to oneself and society, by expecting due regard for itself as a matter of course; and it shows an equally natural regard for others, whether they are of higher or of lower degree. We need all along the line to recover the lost sense of quality and a social order based on quality. Quality is the greatest enemy of any kind of mass-levelling. Socially it means the renunciation of all place-hunting, a break with the cult of the 'star', an open eye both upwards and downwards, especially in the choice of one's more intimate friends, and pleasure in private life as well as courage to enter public life. Culturally it means a return from the newspaper and the radio to the book, from feverish activity to unhurried leisure, from dispersion to concentration, from sensationalism to reflection, from virtuosity to art, from snobbery to modesty, from extravagance to moderation. Quantities are competitive, qualities are complementary.

Sympathy

We must allow for the fact that most people learn wisdom only by personal experience. This explains, first, why so few people are capable of taking precautions in advance – they always fancy that they will somehow or other avoid the danger, till it is too late. Secondly, it explains their insensibility to the sufferings of others; sympathy grows in proportion to the fear of approaching disaster. There is a good deal of excuse on ethical grounds for this attitude. No one wants to meet fate head-on; inward calling and strength for action are acquired only in the actual emergency. No one is responsible for all the injustice and suffering in the world, and no one wants to set himself up as the judge of the world. Psychologically, our lack of imagination, of sensitivity, and of mental alertness is balanced by a steady composure, an ability to go on working, and a great capacity for suffering. But from a Christian point of view, none of these excuses can obscure the fact that the most important factor, large-heartedness, is lacking.

Christ kept himself from suffering till his hour had come, but when it did come he met it as a free man, seized it, and mastered it. Christ, so the scriptures tell us, bore the sufferings of all humanity in his own body as if they were his own – a thought beyond our comprehension – accepting them of his own free will. We are certainly not Christ; we are not called on to redeem the world by our own deeds and sufferings, and we need not try to assume such an impossible burden. We are not lords, but instruments in the hand of the Lord of history; and we can share in other people's sufferings only to a very limited degree. We are not Christ, but if we want to be Christians, we must have some share in Christ's large-heartedness by acting with responsibility and in freedom when the hour of danger comes, and by showing a real sympathy that springs, not from fear, but from the liberating and redeeming love of Christ for all who suffer. Mere waiting and looking on is not Christian behaviour. The Christian is called to sympathy and action, not in the first place by his own sufferings, but by the sufferings of his brethren, for whose sake Christ suffered.

Of suffering

It is infinitely easier to suffer in obedience to a human command than in the freedom of one's own responsibility. It is infinitely easier to suffer with others than to suffer alone. It is infinitely easier to suffer publicly and honourably than apart and ignominiously. It is infinitely easier to suffer through staking one's life than to suffer spiritually. Christ suffered as a free man alone, apart and in ignominy, in body and spirit; and since then many Christians have suffered with him.

Present and future

We used to think that one of the inalienable rights of man was that he should be able to plan both his professional and his private life. That is a thing of the past. The force of circumstances has brought us into a situation where we have to give up being 'anxious about tomorrow' (Matt. 6.34). But it makes all the difference whether we accept this willingly and in faith (as the Sermon on the Mount intends), or under continual constraint. For most people, the compulsory abandonment of planning for the future means that they are forced back into living just for the moment, irresponsibly, frivolously, or resignedly; some few dream longingly of better times to come, and try to forget the present. We find both these courses equally impossible, and there remains for us only the very narrow way, often extremely difficult to find, of living every day as if it were our last, and yet living in faith and responsibility as though there were to be a great future: 'Houses and fields and vineyards shall again be bought in this land' proclaims Jeremiah (32.15), in paradoxical contrast to his prophecies of woe, just before the destruction of the holy city. It is a sign from God and a pledge of a fresh start and a great future, just when all seems black. Thinking and acting for the sake of the coming generation, but being ready to go any day without fear or anxiety – that, in practice, is the spirit in which we are forced to live. It is not easy to be brave and keep that spirit alive, but it is imperative.

Optimism

It is wiser to be pessimistic; it is a way of avoiding disappointment and ridicule, and so wise people condemn optimism. The essence of optimism is not its view of the present, but the fact that it is the inspiration of life and hope when others give in; it enables a man to hold his head high when everything seems to be going wrong; it gives him strength to sustain reverses and yet to claim the future for himself instead of abandoning it to his opponent. It is true that there is a silly, cowardly kind of optimism, which we must condemn. But the optimism that is will for the future should never be despised, even if it is proved wrong a hundred times; it is health and vitality, and the sick man has no business to impugn it. There are people who regard it as frivolous, and some Christians think it impious for anyone to hope and prepare for a better earthly future. They think that the meaning of present events is chaos, disorder, and catastrophe; and in resignation or pious escapism they surrender all responsibility for reconstruction and for future generations. It may be that the day of judgment will dawn tomorrow; in that case, we shall gladly stop working for a better future. But not before.

Insecurity and death

In recent years we have become increasingly familiar with the thought of death. We surprise ourselves by the calmness with which we hear of the death of one of our contemporaries. We cannot hate it as we used to, for we have discovered some good in it, and have almost come to terms with it. Fundamentally we feel that we really belong to death already, and that every new day is a miracle. It would probably not be true to say that we welcome death (although we all know that weariness which we ought to avoid like the plague); we are too inquisitive for that – or, to put it more seriously, we should like to see something more of the meaning of our life's broken fragments. Nor do we try to romanticize death, for life is too great and too precious. Still less do we suppose that danger is the meaning of life – we are not desperate enough for that, and we know too much about the good things that life has to offer, though on the other hand we are only too familiar with life's anxieties and with all the other destructive effects of prolonged personal insecurity. We still love life, but I do not think that death can take us by surprise now. After what we have been through during the war, we hardly dare admit that we should like death to come to us, not accidentally and suddenly through some trivial cause, but in the fullness of life and with everything at stake. It is we ourselves, and not outward circumstances, who make death what it can be, a death freely and voluntarily accepted.

Are we still of any use?

We have been silent witnesses of evil deeds; we have been drenched by many storms; we have learnt the arts of equivocation and pretence; experience has made us suspicious of others and kept us from being truthful and open; intolerable conflicts have worn us down and even made us cynical. Are we still of any use? What we shall need is not geniuses, or cynics, or misanthropes, or clever tacticians, but plain, honest, straightforward men. Will our inward power of resistance be strong enough, and our honesty with ourselves remorseless enough, for us to find our way back to simplicity and straightforwardness?

New Year 1943
Letters and Papers from Prison, 3–17

The despiser of men

God loves man. God loves the world. It is not an ideal man that he loves, but man as he is; not an ideal world, but the real world. What we find abominable in man's opposition to God, what we shrink back from with pain and hostility, the real man, the real world, this is for God the ground for unfathomable love, and it is with this that he unites himself utterly. God becomes man, real man. While we are trying to grow out beyond our manhood, to leave the man behind us, God becomes man and we have to recognize that God wishes us men, too, to be real men. While we are distinguishing the pious from the ungodly, the good from the wicked, the noble from the mean, God makes no distinction at all in his love for the real man. He does not permit us to classify men and the world according to our own standards and to set ourselves up as judges over them. He leads us *ad absurdum* by himself becoming a real man and a companion of sinners and thereby compelling us to become the judges of God. God sides with the real man and with the real world against all their accusers. Together with men and with the world he comes before the judges, so that the judges are now made the accused . . .

The news that God has become man strikes at the very heart of an age in which both the good and the wicked regard either scorn for man or the idolization of man as the highest attainable wisdom. The weaknesses of human nature are displayed more clearly in a time of storm than in the smooth course of more peaceful periods. In the face of totally unexpected threats and opportunities it is fear, desire, irresolution and brutality which reveal themselves as the motives for the actions of the overwhelming majority. At such a time as this it is easy for the tyrannical despiser of men to exploit the baseness of the human heart, nurturing it and calling it by other names. Fear he calls responsibility. Desire he calls keenness. Irresolution becomes solidarity. Brutality becomes masterfulness. Human weaknesses are played upon with unchaste seductiveness, so that meanness and baseness are reproduced and multiplied ever anew. The vilest contempt for mankind goes about its sinister business with the holiest of protestations of devotion to the human cause. And, as the base man grows baser, he becomes

61

an ever more willing and adaptable tool in the hand of the tyrant. The small band of the upright are reviled. Their bravery is called insubordination; their self-control is called pharisaism; their independence arbitrariness and their masterfulness arrogance. For the tyrannical despiser of men popularity is the token of the highest love for mankind. His secret profound mistrust for all human beings he conceals behind words stolen from a true community. In the presence of the crowd he professes to be one of their number, and at the same time he sings his own praises with the most revolting vanity and scorns the rights of every individual. He thinks people stupid, and they become stupid. He thinks them weak, and they become weak. He thinks them criminal, and they become criminal. His most sacred earnestness is a frivolous game. His hearty and worthy solicitude is the most impudent cynicism. In his profound contempt for his fellowmen he seeks the favour of those whom he despises, and the more he does so the more certainly he promotes the deification of his own person by the mob. Contempt for man and idolization of man are close neighbours. But the good man too, no less than the wicked, succumbs to the same temptation to be a despiser of mankind if he sees through all this and withdraws in disgust, leaving his fellow-men to their own devices, and if he prefers to mind his own business rather than to debase himself in public life. Of course, his contempt for mankind is more respectable and upright, but it is also more barren and ineffectual. In the face of God's becoming man the good man's contemptuous attitude cannot be maintained, any more than can the tyrant's. The despiser of men despises what God has loved. Indeed he despises even the figure of the God who has become man . . .

It is only through God's being made man that it is possible to know the real man and not to despise him. The real man can live before God, and we can allow the real man to live before God side by side with ourselves without either despising or deifying him. That is not to say that this is really a value on its own account. It is simply and solely because God has loved the real man and has taken him to himself. The ground for God's love towards man does not lie in man but solely in God himself. And again, the reason why we can live as real men and can love the real man at our side is to be found solely in the incarnation of God, in the unfathomable love of God for man.

Ethics, 52–56

Radicalism and compromise

Two extreme solutions can be given to the problem of the relation of the penultimate with the ultimate in Christian life. It may be solved 'radically' or by means of a compromise; and it is to be noted at once that the compromise solution, too, is an extreme solution.

The radical solution sees only the ultimate, and in it only the complete breaking off of the penultimate. Ultimate and penultimate are here mutually exclusive contraries. Christ is the destroyer and enemy of everything penultimate, and everything penultimate is enmity towards Christ. Christ is the sign that the world is ripe for burning. There are no distinctions. Everything must go to the judgment. There are only two categories: for Christ, and against him. 'He that is not with me is against me' (Matt. 12.30). Everything penultimate in human behaviour is sin and denial. In the face of the approaching end there is for the Christian only the last word and his last conduct. What becomes of the world through this is no longer of any consequence. The Christian bears no responsibility for it, and the world must in any case perish. No matter if the whole order of the world breaks down under the impact of the word of Christ, there must be no holding back. The last word of God, which is a word of mercy, here becomes the icy hardness of the law, which despises and breaks down all resistance.

The other solution is the compromise. Here the last word is on principle set apart from all preceding words. The penultimate retains its right on its own account, and is not threatened or imperilled by the ultimate. The world still stands; the end is not yet here; there are still penultimate things which must be done, in fulfilment of the responsibility for this world which God has created. Account must still be taken of men as they are. The ultimate remains totally on the far side of the everyday; it is thus, in fact, an eternal justification for things as they are; it is the metaphysical purification from the accusation which weighs upon

63

everything that is. The free word of mercy now becomes the law of mercy, which rules over everything penultimate, justifying it and certifying its worth . . .

Radicalism always springs from a conscious or unconscious hatred of what is established. Christian radicalism, no matter whether it consists in withdrawing from the world or in improving the world, arises from hatred of creation. The radical cannot forgive God his creation. He has fallen out with the created world, the Ivan Karamazov, who at the same time makes the figure of the radical Jesus in the legend of the Grand Inquisitor. When evil becomes powerful in the world, it infects the Christian, too, with the poison of radicalism. It is Christ's gift to the Christian that he should be reconciled with the world as it is, but now this reconciliation is accounted a betrayal and denial of Christ. It is replaced by bitterness, suspicion and contempt for men and the world. In the place of the love that believes all, bears all and hopes all, in the place of the love which loves the world in its very wickedness with the love of God (John 3.16), there is now the pharisaical denial of love to evil, and the restriction of love to the closed circle of the devout. Instead of the open church of Jesus Christ, which serves the world till the end, there is now some allegedly primitive Christian ideal of a Church, which in its turn confuses the reality of the living Jesus Christ with the realization of a Christian idea. Thus a world which has become evil succeeds in making the Christians become evil too. It is the same germ that disintegrates the world and that makes the Christians become radical. In both cases it is hatred towards the world, no matter whether the haters are the ungodly or the godly. On both sides it is a refusal of faith in the creation. But devils are not cast out through Beelzebub.

Compromise always springs from hatred of the ultimate. The Christian spirit of compromise arises from hatred of the justification of the sinner by grace alone. The world and life within it have to be protected against this encroachment on their territory. The world must be dealt with solely by means which are of the world. The ultimate has no voice in determining the form of life in the world. Even the raising of the question of the ultimate, even the endeavour to give effect to God's word in its authority for life in the world, is now accounted radicalism and apathy or antipathy towards the established orders of the world and towards the men who are subject to these orders. That freedom from the world which Christ has given to the Christians, as well as the renunciation of the world (I John 2.17), is now denounced as opposition to creation, as unnatural estrangement from the world and from men, and even as hostility towards them. In their place adaptability, even to the point of resignedness, and mere worldy-wise prudence and discretion, are passed off as genuine openness to the world and as genuine Christian charity.

Radicalism hates time, and compromise hates eternity. Radicalism hates patience, and compromise hates decision. Radicalism hates wisdom, and compromise hates simplicity. Radicalism hates moderation and measure, and compromise hates the immeasurable. Radicalism hates the real, and compromise hates the word.

To contrast the two attitudes in this way is to make it sufficiently clear that both alike are opposed to Christ. For in Jesus Christ those things which are here ranged in mutual hostility are one. The question of the Christian life will not, therefore, be decided and answered either by radicalism or by compromise, but only by reference to Jesus Christ himself. In him alone lies the solution for the problem of the relation between the ultimate and the penultimate.

In Jesus Christ we have faith in the incarnate, crucified and risen God. In the incarnation we learn of the love of God for his creation; in the crucifixion we learn of the judgment of God upon all flesh; and in the resurrection we learn of God's will for a new world. There could be no greater error than to tear these three elements apart; for each of them comprises the whole. It is quite wrong to establish a separate theology of the incarnation, a theology of the cross, or a theology of the resurrection, each in opposition to the others, by a misconceived absolutization of one of these parts; it is equally wrong to apply the same procedure to a consideration of the Christian life. A Christian ethic constructed solely on the basis of the incarnation would lead directly to the compromise solution. An ethic which was based solely on the cross or the resurrection of Jesus would fall victim to radicalism and enthusiasm. Only in the unity is the conflict resolved.

Ethics, 103–108

Outline for a book

I should like to write a book of not more than 100 pages, divided into three chapters:
1. A Stocktaking of Christianity
2. The Real Meaning of Christian Faith
3. Conclusions

Chapter 1 to deal with

(*a*) The coming of age of mankind (as already indicated). The safeguarding of life against 'accidents' and 'blows of fate'; even if these cannot be eliminated, the danger can be reduced. Insurance (which, although it lives on 'accidents', seeks to mitigate their effects) as a western phenomenon. The aim: to be independent of nature. Nature was formerly conquered by spiritual means, with us by technical organization of all kinds. Our immediate environment is not nature, as formerly, but organization. But with this protection from nature's menace there arises a new one – through organization itself.

But the spiritual force is lacking. The question is: What protects us against the menace of organization? Man is again thrown back on himself. He has managed to deal with everything, only not with himself. He can insure against everything, only not against man. In the last resort it all turns on man.

(*b*) The religionlessness of man who has come of age. 'God' as a working hypothesis, as a stop-gap for our embarrassments, has become superfluous (as already indicated).

(*c*) The Protestant church: Pietism as a last attempt to maintain evangelical Christianity as a religion; Lutheran orthodoxy, the attempt to rescue the church as an institution for salvation; the Confessing Church: the theology of revelation; a δὸς μοὶ ποῦ στῶ over against the world, involving a 'factual' interest in Christianity; art and science searching for their origin. Generally in the Confessing Church: standing up for the church's 'cause', but little personal faith in Christ. 'Jesus' is disappearing from sight. Sociologically: no effect on the masses – interest confined to the upper and lower middle classes. A heavy incubus of difficult traditional ideas. The decisive factor: the church on the defensive. No taking risks for others.

66

(*d*) Public morals – as shown by sexual behaviour.

Chapter 2

(*a*) God and the secular.

(*b*) Who is God? Not in the first place an abstract belief in God, in his omnipotence etc. That is not a genuine experience of God, but a partial extension of the world. Encounter with Jesus Christ. The experience that a transformation of all human life is given in the fact that 'Jesus is there only for others'. His 'being there for others' is the experience of transcendence. It is only this 'being there for others', maintained till death, that is the ground of his omnipotence, omniscience, and omnipresence. Faith is participation in this being of Jesus (incarnation, cross, and resurrection). Our relation to God is not a 'religious' relationship to the highest, most powerful, and best Being imaginable – that is not authentic transcendence – but our relation to God is a new life in 'existence for others', through participation in the being of Jesus. The transcendental is not infinite and unattainable tasks, but the neighbour who is within reach in any given situation. God in human form – not, as in oriental religions, in animal form, monstrous, chaotic, remote, and terrifying, nor in the conceptual forms of the absolute, metaphysical, infinite, etc., nor yet in the Greek divine-human form of 'man in himself', but 'the man for others', and therefore the Crucified, the man who lives out of the transcendent.

(*c*) Interpretation of biblical concepts on this basis. (Creation, fall, atonement, repentance, faith, the new life, the last things.)

(*d*) Cultus. (Details to follow later, in particular on cultus and 'religion'.)

(*e*) What do we really believe? I mean, believe in such a way that we stake our lives on it? The problem of the Apostles' Creed? 'What *must* I believe?' is the wrong question; antiquated controversies, especially those between the different sects; the Lutheran versus Reformed, and to some extent the Roman Catholic versus Protestant, are now unreal. They may at any time be revived with passion, but they no longer carry conviction. There is no proof of this, and we must simply take it that it is so. All that we can prove is that the faith of the Bible and Christianity does not stand or fall by these issues. Karl Barth and the Confessing Church have encouraged us to entrench ourselves persistently behind the 'faith of the church', and evade the honest question as to what we ourselves really believe. That is why the air is not quite fresh, even in the Confessing Church. To say that it is the church's business, not mine, may be a clerical evasion, and outsiders always regard it as such. It is much the same with the dialectical assertion that I do not control my own faith, and that it is therefore not for me to say what my faith is. There may be a place for all these considerations, but they do not absolve us from the duty of being honest with ourselves. We cannot, like the Roman Catholics, simply identify ourselves with the church. (This, incidentally, explains the popular opinion about Roman Catholics' insincerity.) Well then, what do we really believe? Answer: see (b), (c), and (d).

Chapter 3

Conclusions:

The church is the church only when it exists for others. To make a start, it should give away all its property to those in need. The clergy must live solely on the free-will offerings of their congregations, or possibly engage in some secular calling. The church must share in the secular problems of ordinary human life, not dominating, but helping and serving. It must tell men of every calling what it means to live in Christ, to exist for others. In particular, our own church will have to take the field against the vices of *hubris*, power-worship, envy, and humbug, as the roots of all evil. It will have to speak of moderation, purity, trust, loyalty, constancy, patience, discipline, humility, contentment, and modesty. It must not under-estimate the importance of human example (which has its origin in the humanity of Jesus and is so important in Paul's teaching); it is not abstract argument, but example, that gives its word emphasis and power. (I hope to take up later this subject of 'example' and its place in the New Testament; it is something that we have almost entirely forgotten.) Further: the question of revising the creeds (the Apostles' Creed); revision of Christian apologetics; reform of the training for the ministry and the pattern of clerical life.

All this is very crude and condensed, but there are certain things that I'm anxious to say simply and clearly – things that we so often like to shirk. Whether I shall succeed is another matter, especially if I cannot discuss it with you. I hope it may be of some help for the church's future.

Letters and Papers from Prison, 380–383

The view from below

There remains an experience of incomparable value, namely that we have learned to see the great events of world history from below, from the perspective of those who are excluded, under suspicion, ill-treated, powerless, oppressed and scorned, in short those who suffer. That is the case, provided that at this time bitterness and envy have not eaten away at our hearts; that we look on things great and small, on sorrow and joy, on strength and weakness, with new eyes; that our perception of what is great, human, just and merciful has become clearer, freer, more incorruptible, indeed that personal suffering is a more useful key, a more fruitful principle for opening up the world in thought and action than personal happiness. The important thing is that this perspective from below should not turn into support for those who are eternally discontented, but that we do justice to life in all its dimensions, and thus affirm it, from a higher content which is really beyond 'above' and 'below'.

Around the end of 1942
Gesammelte Schriften II, 441

Confession of guilt

It is a sign of the living presence of Christ that there are men in whom the knowledge of the apostasy from Jesus Christ is kept awake not merely in the sense that this apostasy is observed in others but in the sense that these men themselves confess themselves guilty of this apostasy. They confess their guilt without any sidelong glance at their fellow offenders. Their confession of guilt is strictly exclusive in that it takes all guilt upon itself. Wherever there is still a weighing up and calculation of guilt, there the sterile morality of self-justification usurps the place of the confession of guilt which is made in the presence of the form of Christ. Not the individual misdeeds but the form of Christ is the origin of the confession of guilt, and for that reason the confession is not unconditional and entire; for Christ subdues us in no other way more utterly than by his having taken our guilt upon himself unconditionally and entirely, declaring himself guilty of our guilt and freeing us from its burden. The sight of this grace of Christ blots out entirely the sight of the guilt of other men and compels a man to fall upon his knees before Christ and to confess *mea culpa*, *mea maxima culpa*.

With this confession the entire guilt of the world falls upon the church, upon the Christians, and since this guilt is not denied here, but is confessed, there arises the possibility of forgiveness. In a way which is totally incomprehensible to the moralist there is no seeking for the actual guilty party; there is no demand for a condign expiation of the guilt, punishment of the wicked and reward of the good. The wicked man is not charged with his wickedness, in the sense of the apocalyptic saying: 'He that is unjust, let him be unjust still' (Rev. 22.11). It is men who take all, really all, guilt upon themselves, not in some heroic resolve of sacrifice, but simply because they are overwhelmed by their own, their very own, guilt towards Christ, so that at this moment they can no longer think of imposing retributive justice on the 'chief offenders' but only of the forgiveness of their own great guilt.

First of all, is the entirely personal sin of the individual which is recognized here as a source of pollution for the community. Even the most secret sin of the individual is defilement and destruction of the body of Christ (I Cor. 6.15). From the desires that are in our bodily members come murder and envy, strife and war (James 4.1ff.). If my share in this is so small as to seem negligible, that still cannot set my mind at rest; for now it is not a matter of apportioning the blame, but I must acknowledge that precisely my sin is to blame for all. I am guilty of uncontrolled desire. I am guilty of cowardly silence at a time when I ought to have spoken. I am guilty of hypocrisy and untruthfulness in the face of force. I have been lacking in compassion and I have denied the poorest of my brethren. I am guilty of disloyalty and of apostasy from Christ. What does it matter to you whether others are guilty too? I can excuse any sin of another, but my own sin alone remains guilt which I can never excuse. It is not a morbidly egotistical distortion of reality, but it is the essential character of a genuine confession of guilt that it is incapable of apportioning blame and pleading a case, but is rather the acknowledgment of one's own sin of Adam. And it is senseless to try to oppose this acknowledgment with an argument *ad absurdum* by pointing out that there are innumerable individuals each of whom must in this way be conscious of being to blame for the whole. For indeed these innumerable individuals are united in the collective personality of the church. It is in them and through them that the church confesses and acknowledges her guilt.

The church confesses that she has not proclaimed often and clearly enough her message of the one God who has revealed himself for all times in Jesus Christ and who suffers no other gods beside himself. She confesses her timidity, her evasiveness, her dangerous concessions. She has often been untrue to her office of guardianship and to her office of comfort. And through this she has often denied to the outcast and to the despised the compassion which she owes them. She was silent when she should have cried out because the blood of the innocent was crying aloud to heaven. She has failed to speak the right word in the right way and at the right time. She has not resisted to the uttermost the apostasy of faith, and she has brought upon herself the guilt of the godlessness of the masses.

The church confesses that she has taken in vain the name of Jesus Christ, for she has been ashamed of this name before the world and she has not striven forcefully enough against the misuse of this name for an evil purpose. She has stood by while violence and wrong were being committed under cover of this name. And indeed she has left uncontradicted, and has thereby abetted, even open mockery of the most holy name. She knows that God will not leave unpunished one who takes his name in vain as she does.

The church confesses herself guilty of the loss of the Sabbath day, of the withering away of her public worship, and of the contemptuous neglect of Sunday as a day of rest. She has incurred the guilt of restlessness and disquiet, and also of the exploitation of labour even beyond the working weekday, because her preaching of Jesus Christ has been feeble and her public worship has been lifeless.

The church confesses herself guilty of the collapse of parental authority. She offered no resistance to contempt for age and idolization of youth, for she was afraid of losing youth, and with it the future. As though her future belonged to youth! She has not dared to proclaim the divine authority and dignity of parenthood in the face of the revolution of youth, and in a very earthly way she has tried 'to keep up with the young'. She has thus rendered herself guilty of the breaking up of countless families, the betrayal of fathers by their children, the self-deification of youth, and the abandonment of youth to the apostasy from Christ.

The church confesses that she has witnessed the lawless application of brutal force, the physical and spiritual suffering of countless innocent people, oppression, hatred and murder, and that she has not raised her voice on behalf of the victims and has not found ways to hasten to their aid. She is guilty of the deaths of the weakest and most defenceless brothers of Jesus Christ.

The church confesses that she has found no word of advice and assistance in the face of the dissolution of all order in the relation between the sexes. She has found no strong and effective answer to the contempt for chastity and to the proclamation of sexual libertinism. All she has achieved has been an occasional expression of moral indignation. She has thus rendered herself guilty of the loss of the purity and soundness of youth. She has failed to proclaim with sufficient emphasis that our bodies belong to the Body of Christ.

The church confesses that she has witnessed in silence the spoliation and exploitation of the poor and the enrichment and corruption of the strong.

The church confesses herself guilty towards the countless victims of calumny, denunciation and defamation. She has not convicted the slanderer of his wrongdoing, and she has thereby abandoned the slandered to his fate.

The church confesses that she has desired security, peace and quiet, possessions and honour, to which she had no right, and that in this way she has not bridled the desires of men but has stimulated them still further.

The church confesses herself guilty of breaking all ten commandments, and in this she confesses her defection from Christ. She has not borne witness to the truth of God in such a manner that all pursuit of truth, all science, can perceive that it has its origin in this truth. She has not proclaimed the justice of God in such a manner that all true justice must see in it the origin of its own essential nature. She has not succeeded in making the providence of God a matter of such certain belief that all human economy must regard it as the source from which it receives its task. By her own silence she has rendered herself guilty of the decline in responsible action, in bravery in the defence of a cause, and in willingness to suffer for what is known to be right. She bears the guilt of the defection of the governing authority from Christ.

Is this saying too much? Will some entirely blameless people stand up at this point and try to prove that it is not the church which is guilty but the others? Are there perhaps some churchmen who would reject all this as mere insulting abuse, who set themselves up to be more competent judges of the world, and who weigh up and apportion the guilt this way and that? Was not the church hindered and tied on all sides? Did not the entire secular force stand against her? Had the church the right to jeopardize her last remaining asset, her public worship and her parish life, by taking up the struggle against the anti-Christian powers? This is the voice of unbelief, which sees in the confession of guilt only a dangerous moral derogation and which fails to see that the confession of guilt is the re-attainment of the form of Jesus Christ who bore the sin of the world. For indeed the free confession of guilt is not something which can be done or left undone at will. It is the emergence of the form of Jesus Christ in the church. Either the church must willingly undergo this transformation, or else she must cease to be the church of Christ. If anyone stifles or corrupts the church's confession of guilt, his guilt towards Christ is beyond hope.

By her confession of guilt the church does not exempt men from their own confession of guilt, but she calls them in into the fellowship of the confession of guilt. Apostate humanity can endure before Christ only if it has fallen under the sentence of Christ. It is to this judgment that the church summons all those who hear her message.

Ethics, 90–95

Deputyship

The fact that responsibility is fundamentally a matter of deputyship is demonstrated most clearly in those circumstances in which a man is directly obliged to act in the place of other men, for example as a father, as a statesman or as a teacher. The father acts for the children, working for them, caring for them, interceding, fighting and suffering for them. Thus in a real sense he is their deputy. He is not an isolated individual, but he combines in himself the selves of a number of human beings. Any attempt to live as though he were alone is a denial of the actual fact of his responsibility. He cannot evade the responsibility which is laid on him with his paternity. This reality shatters the fiction that the subject, the performer, of all ethical conduct is the isolated individual. Not the individual in isolation but the responsible man is the subject, the agent, with whom ethical reflexion must concern itself. This principle is not affected by the extent of the responsibility assumed, whether it be for a single human being, for a community or for whole groups of communities. No man can altogether escape responsibility, and this means that no man can avoid deputyship. Even the solitary lives as a deputy, and indeed quite especially so, for his life is lived in deputyship for man as man, for mankind as a whole. And, in fact, the concept of responsibility for oneself possesses a meaning only in so far as it refers to the responsibility which I bear with respect to myself as a man, that is to say, because I am a man. Responsibility for oneself is in truth responsibility with respect to the man, and that means responsibility with respect to mankind. The fact that Jesus lived without the special responsibility of a marriage, of a family or of a profession, does not by any means set him outside the field of responsibility; on the contrary, it makes all the clearer his responsibility and his deputyship for all men. Here we come already to the underlying basis of everything that has been said so far. Jesus, life, our life, lived in deputyship for us as the incarnate Son of God, and that is why through him all human life is in essence a life of deputyship. Jesus was not the individual, desiring to achieve a perfection of his own, but he lived only as the one who has taken up into himself and who bears within himself the selves of all men. All his living, his action and his dying was deputyship. In him there is fulfilled what the living, the action and the suffering of men ought to be. In this real deputyship which constitutes his human existence he is the responsible person *par excellence*. Because he is life all life is determined by him to be deputyship. Whether or not life resists, it is now always deputyship, for life or for death, just as the father is always a father, for good or for evil.

Deputyship, and therefore also responsibility, lies only in the complete surrender of one's own life to the other man. Only the selfless man lives responsibly, and this means that only the selfless man *lives*. Wherever the divine 'yes' and 'no' become one in man, there is responsible living. Selflessness in responsibility is so complete that here we may find the fulfilment of Goethe's saying about the man of action being always without conscience. The life of deputyship is open to two abuses; one may set up one's own ego as an absolute, or one may set up the other man as an absolute. In the first case the relation of responsibility leads to forcible exploitation and tyranny; this springs from a failure to recognize that only the selfless man can act responsibly. In the second case what is made absolute is the welfare of the other man, the man towards whom I am responsible, and all other responsibilities are neglected. From this there arises arbitrary action which makes mock of the responsibility to God who in Jesus Christ is the God of all men. In both these cases there is a denial of the origin, the essence and the goal of responsible life in Jesus Christ, and responsibility itself is set up as a self-made abstract idol.

Responsibility, as life and action in deputyship, is essentially a relation of man to man. Christ became man, and he therefore bore responsibility and deputyship for men. There is also a responsibility for things, conditions and values, but only in conjunction with the strict observance of the original, essential and purposive determination of all things, conditions, and values through Christ (John 1.3), the incarnate God. Through Christ the world of things and of values is once more directed towards mankind as it was in the creation. It is only within these limits that there is a legitimate sense in speaking, as is often done, about responsibility for a thing or for a cause. Beyond these limits it is dangerous, for it serves to reverse the whole order of life, making things the masters of men. There is a devotion to the cause of truth, goodness, justice and beauty which would be profaned if one were to ask what is the moral of it, and which indeed itself makes it abundantly clear that the highest values must be subservient to man. But there is also a deification of all these values which has no connexion at all with responsibility; it springs from a demoniacal possession which destroys the man in sacrificing him to the idol. 'Responsibility for a thing' does not mean its utilization for man and consequently the abuse of its essential nature, but it means the essential directing of it towards man. Thus that narrow pragmatism is entirely excluded which, in Schiller's words, 'makes a milch-cow of the goddess' when that which has value in itself is in a direct and short-sighted manner subordinated to human utility. The world of things attains to its full liberty and depth only when it is grasped in its original, essential and purposive relevance to the world of persons; for, as St Paul expresses it, the earnest expectation of the creature waits for the manifestation of the glory of the children of God; and indeed the creature itself shall be delivered from the bondage of corruption (which also consists in its own false self-deification) into the glorious liberty of the children of God (Rom. 8.19–21).

Ethics, 194–197

The acceptance of guilt

From what has just been said it emerges that the structure of responsible action includes both readiness to accept guilt and freedom.

When we once more turn our attention to the origin of all responsibility it becomes clear to us what we are to understand by acceptance of guilt. Jesus is not concerned with the proclamation and realization of new ethical ideals; he is not concerned with himself being good (Matt. 19.17); he is concerned solely with love for the real man, and for that reason he is able to enter into the fellowship of the guilt of men and to take the burden of their guilt upon himself. Jesus does not desire to be regarded as the only perfect one at the expense of men; he does not desire to look down on mankind as the only guiltless one while mankind goes to its ruin under the weight of its guilt; he does not wish that some idea of a new man should triumph amid the wreckage of a humanity whose guilt has destroyed it. He does not wish to acquit himself of the guilt under which men die. A love which left man alone in his guilt would not be love for the real man. As one who acts responsibly in the historical existence of men Jesus becomes guilty. It must be emphasized that it is solely his love which makes him incur guilt. From his selfless love, from his freedom from sin, Jesus enters into the guilt of men and takes this guilt upon himself. Freedom from sin and the question of guilt are inseparable in him. It is as the one who is without sin that Jesus takes upon himself the guilt of his brothers, and it is under the burden of this guilt that he shows himself to be without sin. In this Jesus Christ, who is guilty without sin, lies the origin of every action of responsible deputyship. If it is responsible action, if it is action which is concerned solely and entirely with the other man, if it arises from selfless love for the real man who is our brother, then, precisely because this is so, it cannot wish to shun the fellowship of human guilt. Jesus took upon himself the guilt of all men, and for that reason every man who acts responsibly becomes guilty. If any man tries to escape guilt in responsibility he detaches himself from the ultimate reality of human existence, and what is more he cuts himself off from the redeeming mystery of Christ's bearing guilt without sin and he has no share in the divine justification which lies upon this event. He sets his own personal innocence above his responsibility for men, and he is blind to the more irredeemable guilt which he incurs precisely in this; he is blind also to the fact that real innocence shows itself precisely in a man's entering into the fellowship of guilt for the sake of other men. Through Jesus Christ it becomes an essential part of responsible action that the man who is without sin loves selflessly and for that reason incurs guilt.

Ethics, 209f.

Conscience

There is a reply to all this which undeniably commands respect. It comes from the high authority of conscience; for conscience is unwilling to sacrifice its integrity to any other value, and it therefore refuses to incur guilt for the sake of another man. Responsibility for our neighbour is cut short by the inviolable call of conscience. A responsibility which would oblige a man to act against his conscience would carry within it its own condemnation. In what respects is this true and in what respects is it false?

It is true that it can never be advisable to act against one's own conscience. All Christian ethics is agreed in this. But what does that mean? Conscience comes from a depth which lies beyond a man's own will and his own reason and it makes itself heard as the call of human existence to unity with itself. Conscience comes as an indictment of the loss of this unity and as a warning against the loss of one's self. Primarily it is directed not towards a particular kind of doing but towards a particular mode of being. It protests against a doing which imperils the unity of this being with itself.

So long as conscience can be formally defined in these terms it is extremely inadvisable to act against its authority; disregard for the call of conscience will necessarily entail the destruction of one's own being, not even a purposeful surrender of it; it will bring about the decline and collapse of a human existence. Action against one's own conscience runs parallel with suicidal action against one's own life, and it is not by chance that the two often go together. Responsible action which did violence to conscience in this formal sense would indeed be reprehensible.

But that is not by any means the end of the question. The call of conscience arises from the imperilling of a man's unity with himself, and it is therefore now necessary to ask what constitutes this unity. The first constituent is the man's own ego in its claim to be 'like God', *sicut deus*, in the knowledge of good and evil. The call of conscience in natural man is the attempt on the part of the ego to justify itself in its knowledge of good and evil before God, before men and before itself, and to secure its own continuance in this self-justification. Finding no firm support in its own contingent individuality the ego traces its own derivation back to a universal law of good and seeks to achieve unity with itself in conformity with this law. Thus the call of conscience has its origin and its goal in the autonomy of a man's own ego. A man's purpose in obeying this call is on each occasion anew that he should himself once more realize this autonomy which has its origin beyond his own will and knowledge 'in Adam'. Thus in his conscience he continues to be bound by a law of his own finding, a law which may assume different concrete forms but which he can transgress only at the price of losing his own self.

We can now understand that the great change takes place at the moment when the unity of human existence ceases to consist in its autonomy and is found, through the miracle of faith, beyond the man's own ego and its law, in Jesus Christ. The form of this change in the point of unity has an exact analogy in the secular sphere. When the national socialist says 'My conscience is Adolf Hitler' that, too, is an attempt to find a foundation for the unity of his own ego somewhere beyond himself. The consequence of this is the surrender of one's autonomy for the sake of an unconditional heteronomy, and this in turn is possible only if the other man, the man to whom I look for the unity of my life, fulfils the function of a redeemer for me. This, then, provides an extremely direct and significant parallel to the Christian truth, and at the same time an extremely direct and significant contrast with it.

When Christ, true God and true man, has become the point of unity of my existence, conscience will indeed still formally be the call of my actual being to unity with myself, but this unity cannot now be realized by means of a return to the autonomy which I derive from the law; it must be realized in fellowship with Jesus Christ. Natural conscience, no matter how strict and rigorous it may be, is now seen to be the most ungodly self-justification, and it is overcome by the conscience which is set free in Jesus Christ and which summons me to unity with myself in Jesus Christ. Jesus Christ has become my conscience. This means that I can now find unity with myself only in the surrender of my ego to God and to men. The origin and the goal of my conscience is not a law but it is the living God and the living man as he confronts me in Jesus Christ.

Ethics, 211ff.

What is meant by 'telling the truth'?

From the moment in our lives at which we learn to speak we are taught that what we say must be true. What does this mean? What is meant by 'telling the truth'? What does it demand of us?

It is clear that in the first place it is our parents who regulate our relation to themselves by this demand for truthfulness; consequently, in the sense in which our parents intend it, this demand applies strictly only within the family circle. It is also to be noted that the relation which is expressed in this demand cannot simply be reversed. The truthfulness of a child towards his parents is essentially different from that of the parents towards their child. The life of the small child lies open before the parents, and what the child says should reveal to them everything that is hidden and secret, but in the converse relationship this cannot possibly be the case. Consequently, in the matter of truthfulness, the parents' claim on the child is different from the child's claim on the parents.

From this it emerges already that 'telling the truth' means something different according to the particular situation in which one stands. Account must be taken of one's relationships at each particular time. The question must be asked whether and in what way a man is entitled to demand truthful speech of others. Speech between parents and children is, in the nature of the case, different from speech between man and wife, between friends, between teacher and pupil, government and subject, friend and foe, and in each case the truth which this speech conveys is also different.

It will at once be objected that one does not owe truthful speech to this or that individual man, but solely to God. This objection is correct so long as it is not forgotten that God is not a general principle, but the living God who has set me in a living life and who demands service of me within this living life. If one speaks of God one must not simply disregard the actual given world in which one lives; for if one does that one is not speaking of the God who entered into the world in Jesus Christ, but rather of some metaphysical idol. And it is precisely this which is determined by the way in which, in my actual concrete life with all its manifold relationships, I give effect to the truthfulness which I owe to God. The truthfulness which we owe to God must assume a concrete form in the world. Our speech must be truthful, not in principle but concretely. A truthfulness which is not concrete is not truthful before God.

'Telling the truth', therefore, is not solely a matter of moral character; it is also a matter of correct appreciation of real situations and of serious reflection upon them. The more complex the actual situations of a man's life, the more responsible and the more difficult will be his task of 'telling the truth'. The child stands in only one vital relationship, his relationship to his parents, and he, therefore, still has nothing to consider and weigh up. The next environment in which he is placed, his school, already brings with it the first difficulty. From the educational point of view it is, therefore, of the very greatest importance that parents, in some way which we cannot discuss here, should make their children understand the differences between these various circles in which they are to live and the differences in their responsibilities.

Telling the truth is, therefore, something which must be learnt. This will sound very shocking to anyone who thinks that it must all depend on moral character and that if this is blameless the rest is child's play. But the simple fact is that the ethical cannot be detached from reality, and consequently continual progress in learning to appreciate reality is a necessary ingredient in ethical action. In the question with which we are now concerned, action consists of speaking. The real is to be expressed in words. That is what constitutes truthful speech. And this inevitably raises the question of the 'how?' of these words. It is a question of knowing the right word on each occasion. Finding this word is a matter of long, earnest and ever more advanced effort on the basis of experience and knowledge of the real. If one is to say how a thing really is, i.e. if one is to speak truthfully, one's gaze and one's thought must be directed towards the way in which the real exists in God and through God and for God.

To restrict this problem of truthful speech to certain particular cases of conflict is superficial. Every word I utter is subject to the requirement that it shall be true. Quite apart from the veracity of its contents, the relation between myself and another man which is expressed in it is in itself either true or untrue. I can speak flatteringly or presumptuously or hypocritically without uttering a material untruth; yet my words are nevertheless untrue, because I am disrupting and destroying the reality of the relationship between man and wife, superior and subordinate, etc. An individual utterance is always part of a total reality which seeks expression in this utterance. If my utterance is to be truthful it must in each case be different according to whom I am addressing, who is questioning me, and what I am speaking about. The truthful word is not in itself constant, it is as much alive as life itself. If it is detached from life and from its reference to the concrete other man, if 'the truth is told' without taking into account to whom it is addressed, then the truth has only the appearance of truth, but it lacks its essential character.

It is only the cynic who claims 'to speak the truth' at all times and in all places to all men in the same way, but who, in fact, displays nothing but a lifeless image of the truth. He dons the halo of the fanatical devotee of truth who can make no allowance for human weaknesses; but, in fact, he is destroying the living truth between men. He wounds shame, desecrates mystery, breaks confidence, betrays the community in which he lives, and laughs arrogantly at the devastation he has wrought and at the human weakness which 'cannot bear the truth'. He says truth is destructive and demands its victims, and he feels like a god above these feeble creatures and does not know that he is serving Satan.

There is a truth which is of Satan. Its essence is that under the semblance of truth it denies everything that is real. It lives upon hatred of the real and of the world which is created and loved by God. It pretends to be executing the judgment of God upon the fall of the real. God's truth judges created things out of love, and Satan's truth judges them out of envy and hatred. God's truth has become flesh in the world and is alive in the real, but Satan's truth is the death of all reality.

The concept of living truth is dangerous, and it gives rise to the suspicion that the truth can and may be adapted to each particular situation in a way which completely destroys the idea of truth and narrows the gap between truth and falsehood, so that the two become indistinguishable. Moreover, what we are saying about the necessity for discerning the real may be mistakenly understood as meaning that it is by adopting a calculating or schoolmasterly attitude towards the other man that I shall decide what proportion of the truth I am prepared to tell him. It is important that this danger should be kept in view. Yet the only possible way of countering it is by means of attentive discerning of the particular contents and limits which the real itself imposes on one's utterance in order to make it a truthful one. The dangers which are involved in the concept of living truth must never impel one to abandon this concept in favour of the formal and cynical concept of truth.

We must try to make this clear. Every utterance or word lives and has its home in a particular environment. The word in the family is different from the word in business or in public. The word which has come to life in the warmth of a personal relationship is frozen to death in the cold air of public existence. The word of command, which has its habitat in public service, would sever the bonds of mutual confidence if it were spoken in the family. Each word must have its own place and keep to it. It is a consequence of the wide diffusion of the public word through the newspapers and the wireless that the essential character and the limits of the various different words are no longer clearly felt and that, for example, the special quality of the personal word is almost entirely destroyed. Genuine words are replaced by idle chatter. Words no longer possess any weight. There is too much talk. And when the limits of the various words are obliterated, when words become rootless and homeless, then the word loses truth, and then indeed there must almost inevitably be lying. When the various orders of life no longer respect one another, words become untrue. For example, a teacher asks a child in front of the class whether it is true that his father often comes home drunk. It is true, but the child denies it. The teacher's question has placed him in a situation for which he is not yet prepared. He feels only that what is taking place is an unjustified interference in the order of the family and that he must oppose it. What goes on in the family is not for the ears of the class in school. The family has its own secret and must preserve it. The teacher has failed to respect the reality of this institution. The child ought now to find a way of answering which would comply with both the rule of the family and the rule of the school. But he is not yet able to do this. He lacks experience, knowledge, and the ability to express himself in the right way. As a simple no to the teacher's question the child's answer is certainly untrue; yet at the same time it nevertheless gives expression to the truth that the family is an institution *sui generis* and that the teacher had no right to interfere in it. The child's answer can indeed be called a lie; yet this lie contains more truth, that is to say, it is more in accordance with reality than would have been the case if the child had betrayed his father's weakness in front of the class. According to the measure of his knowledge, the child acted correctly. The blame for the lie falls back entirely upon the teacher. An experienced man in the same position as the child would have been able to correct the questioner's error while at the same time avoiding a formal untruth in his answer, and he would thus have found the 'right word'. The lies of children, and of the inexperienced people in general, are often to be ascribed to the fact that these people are faced with situations which they do not fully understand. Consequently, since the term lie is quite properly understood as meaning something which is quite simply and utterly wrong, it is perhaps unwise to generalize and extend the use of this term so that it can be applied to every statement which is formally untrue. Indeed here already it becomes apparent how very difficult it is to say what actually constitutes a lie.

The usual definition of the lie as a conscious discrepancy between thought and speech is completely inadequate. This would include, for example, even the most harmless April-fool joke. The concept of the 'jocular lie', which is maintained in Catholic moral theology, takes away from the lie its characteristic features of seriousness and malice (and, conversely, takes away from the joke its characteristic features of harmless playfulness and freedom); no more unfortunate concept could have been thought of. Joking has nothing whatever to do with lying, and the two must not be reduced to a common denominator. If it is now asserted that a lie is a deliberate deception of another man to his detriment, then this would also include, for example, the necessary deception of the enemy in war or in similar situations. If this sort of conduct is called lying, the lie thereby acquires a moral sanction and justification which conflicts in every possible way with the accepted meaning of the term. The first conclusion to be drawn from this is that the lie cannot be defined in formal terms as a discrepancy between thought and speech. This discrepancy is not even a necessary ingredient of the lie. There is a way of speaking which is in this respect entirely correct and unexceptionable, but which is, nevertheless, a lie. This is exemplified when a notorious liar for once tells 'the truth' in order to mislead, and when an apparently correct statement contains some deliberate ambiguity or deliberately omits the essential part of the truth. Even a deliberate silence may constitute a lie, although this is not by any means necessarily the case.

From these considerations it becomes evident that the essential character of the lie is to be found at a far deeper level than in the discrepancy between thought and speech. One might say that the man who stands behind the word makes his word a lie or a truth. But even this is not enough; for the lie is something objective and must be defined accordingly. Jesus calls Satan 'the father of the lie' (John 8.44). The lie is primarily the denial of God as he has evidenced himself to the world. 'Who is a liar but he that denieth that Jesus is the Christ? (I John 2.22). The lie is a contradiction of the word of God, which God has spoken in Christ, and upon which creation is founded. Consequently the lie is the denial, the negation and the conscious and deliberate destruction of the reality which is created by God and which consists in God, no matter whether this purpose is achieved by speech or by silence. The assigned purpose of our words, in unity with the word of God, is to express the real, as it exists in God; and the assigned purpose of our silence is to signify the limit which is imposed upon our words by the real as it exists in God.

In our endeavours to express the real we do not encounter this as a consistent whole, but in a condition of disruption and inner contradiction which has need of reconciliation and healing. We find ourselves simultaneously embedded in various different orders of the real, and our words, which strive towards the reconciliation and healing of the real, are nevertheless repeatedly drawn in into the prevalent disunion and conflict. They can indeed fulfil their assigned purpose of expressing the real, as it is in God, only by taking up into themselves both the inner contradiction and the inner consistency of the real. If the words of men are to be true they must deny neither the Fall nor God's word of creation and reconciliation, the word in which all disunion is overcome. For the cynic the truthfulness of his words will consist in his giving expression on each separate occasion to the particular reality as he thinks he perceives it, without reference to the totality of the real; and precisely through this he completely destroys the real. Even if his words have the superficial appearance of correctness, they are untrue. 'That which is far off, and exceeding deep; who can find it out?' (Eccl. 7.24).

How can I speak the truth?

1. By perceiving who causes me to speak and what entitles me to speak.

85

2. By perceiving the place at which I stand.

3. By relating to this context the object about which I am making some assertion.

It is tacitly assumed in these rules that all speech is subject to certain conditions; speech does not accompany the natural course of life in a continual stream, but it has its place, its time and its task, and consequently also its limits.

Ethics, 326–333

Thoughts on the day of the baptism of Dietrich Wilhelm Rüdiger Bethge

You are the first of a new generation in our family, and therefore the oldest representative of your generation. You will have the priceless advantage of spending a good part of your life with the third and fourth generation that went before you. Your great-grandfather will be able to tell you, from his own personal memories, of people who were born in the eighteenth century; and one day, long after the year 2000, you will be the living bridge over which your descendants will get an oral tradition of more than 250 years – all this *sub conditione Jacobea*, 'if the Lord wills'. So your birth provides us with a suitable occasion to reflect on the changes that time brings, and to try to scan the outlines of the future.

The three names that you bear refer to three houses with which your life is, and always should be, inseparably connected. Your grandfather on your father's side lived in a country parsonage. A simple, healthy life, with wide intellectual interests, joy in the most homely things, a natural and unaffected interest in ordinary people and their work, a capacity for self-help in practical things, and a modesty grounded in spiritual contentment – those are the earthly values which were at home in the country parsonage, and which you will meet in your father. In all the circumstances of life you will find them a firm basis for living together with other people, and for achieving real success and inward happiness.

The urban middle-class culture embodied in the home of your mother's parents has led to pride in public service, intellectual achievement and leadership, and a deep-rooted sense of duty towards a great heritage and cultural tradition. This will give you, even before you are aware of it, a way of thinking and acting which you can never lose without being untrue to yourself.

It was a kindly thought of your parents that you should be known by the name of your great-uncle, who is a pastor and a great friend of your father's; he is at present sharing the fate of many other good Germans and Protestant Christians, and so he has only been able to participate at a distance in your parents' wedding and in your own birth and baptism, but he looks forward to your future with great confidence and cheerful hope. He is striving to keep up the spirit – as far as he understands it – that is embodied in his parents' (your great-grandparents') home. He takes it as a good omen for your future that it was in that home that your parents got to know each other, and he hopes that one day you will be thankful for its spirit and draw on the strength that it gives.

By the time you have grown up, the old country parsonage and the old town villa will belong to a vanished world. But the old spirit, after a time of misunderstanding and weakness, withdrawal and recovery, preservation and rehabilitation, will produce new forms. To be deeply rooted in the soil of the past makes life harder, but it also makes it richer and more vigorous. There are in human life certain fundamental truths to which men will always return sooner or later. So there is no need to hurry; we have to be able to wait. 'God seeks what has been driven away' (Eccles. 3.15).

In the revolutionary times ahead the greatest gift will be to know the security of a good home. It will be a bulwark against all dangers from within and without. The time when children broke away in arrogance from their parents will be past. Children will be drawn into their parents' protection, and they will seek refuge, counsel, peace, and enlightenment. You are lucky to have parents who know at first hand what it means to have a parental home in stormy times. In the general impoverishment of intellectual life you will find your parents' home a storehouse of spiritual values and a source of intellectual stimulation. Music, as your parents understand and practise it, will help to dissolve your perplexities and purify your character and sensibility, and in times of care and

87

sorrow will keep a ground-bass of joy alive in you. Your parents will soon be teaching you to help yourself and never to be afraid of soiling your hands. The piety of your home will not be noisy or loquacious, but it will teach you to say your prayers, to fear and love God above everything, and to do the will of Jesus Christ. 'My son, keep your father's commandment, and forsake not your mother's teaching. Bind them upon your heart always; tie them about your neck. When you walk, they will lead you; when you lie down, they will watch over you; and when you awake, they will talk with you' (Prov. 6.20–22). 'Today salvation has come to this house' (Luke 19.9).

I wish you could grow up in the country; but it will not be the countryside in which your father grew up. People used to think that the big cities offered the fullest kind of life and lots of pleasure, and they used to flock to them as though to a festival; but those cities have now brought on themselves death and dying, with all imaginable horrors, and have become fearsome places from which women and children have fled. The age of big cities on our continent seems to have come to an end. According to the Bible, Cain founded the first city. It may be that a few world metropolises will survive, but their brilliance, however alluring it may be, will in any case have something uncanny about it for a European. On the other hand, the flight from the cities will mean that the countryside is completely changed. The peace and seclusion of country life have already been largely undermined by the radio, the car, and the telephone, and by the spread of bureaucracy into almost every department of life; and now if millions of people who can no longer endure the pace and the demands of city life are moving into the country, and if entire industries are dispersed into rural areas, then the urbanization of the country will go ahead fast, and the whole basic structure of life there will be changed. The village of thirty years ago no more exists today than the idyllic South Sea island. In spite of man's longing for peace and solitude, these will be difficult to find. But with all these changes, it will be an advantage to have under one's feet a plot of land from which to draw the resources of a new, natural, unpretentious, and contented day's work and evening's leisure. 'There is great gain in godliness and contentment; . . . if we have food and clothing, with these we shall be content.' (I Tim. 6.6f.). 'Give me neither poverty nor riches; feed me with the food that is needful for me, lest I be full, and deny thee, and say, "Who is the Lord?", or lest I be poor, and steal, and profane the name of my God' (Prov. 30.8f.). 'Flee from the midst of Babylon . . . She was not healed . . . Forsake her, and let us go each to his own country' (Jer. 51.6,9).

We have grown up with the experience of our parents and grandparents that a man can and must plan, develop, and shape his own life, and that life has a purpose, about which a man must make up his mind, and which he must then pursue with all his strength. But we have learnt by experience that we cannot plan even for the coming day, that what we have built up is being destroyed overnight, and that our life, in contrast to that of our parents, has become formless or even fragmentary. In spite of that, I can only say that I have no wish to live in any other time than our own, even though it is so inconsiderate of our outward well-being. We realize more clearly than formerly that the world lies under the wrath and grace of God. We read in Jer. 45: 'Thus says the Lord: Behold, what I have built I am breaking down, and what I have planted I am plucking up . . . And do you seek great things for yourself? Seek them not; for, behold, I am bringing evil upon all flesh; . . . but I will give your life as a prize of war in all places to which you may go.' If we can save our souls unscathed out of the wreckage of our material possessions, let us be satisfied with that. If the Creator destroys his own handiwork, what right have we to lament the destruction of ours? It will be the task of our generation, not to 'seek great things', but to save and preserve our souls out of the chaos, and to realize that it is the only thing we can carry as a 'prize' from the burning building. 'Keep your heart with all vigilance; for from it flows the spring of life' (Prov. 4.23). We shall have to keep our lives rather than shape them, to hope rather than plan, to hold out rather than march forward. But we do want to preserve for you, the rising generation, what will make it possible for you to plan, build up, and shape a new and better life.

We have spent too much time in thinking, supposing that if we

89

weigh in advance the possibilities of any action, it will happen automatically. We have learnt, rather too late, that action comes, not from thought, but from a readiness for responsibility. For you thought and action will enter on a new relationship; your thinking will be confined to your responsibilities in action. With us thought was often the luxury of the onlooker; with you it will be entirely subordinated to action. 'Not every one who *says* to me, "Lord, Lord"', shall enter the kingdom of heaven, but he who *does* the will of my Father who is in heaven', said Jesus (Matt. 7.21).

For the greater part of our lives pain was a stranger to us. To be as free as possible from pain was unconsciously one of our guiding principles. Niceties of feeling, sensitivity to our own and other people's pain are at once the strength and the weakness of our way of life. From its early days your generation will be tougher and closer to real life, for you will have had to endure privation and pain, and your patience will have been greatly tried. 'It is good for a man that he bear the yoke in his youth' (Lam. 3.27).

We thought we could make our way in life with reason and justice, and when both failed, we felt that we were at the end of our tether. We have constantly exaggerated the importance of reason and justice in the course of history. You, who are growing up in a world war which ninety per cent of mankind did not want, but for which they have to risk losing their goods and their lives, are learning from childhood that the world is controlled by forces against which reason can do nothing; and so you will be able to cope with those forces more successfully. In our lives the 'enemy' did not really exist. You know that you have enemies and friends, and you know what they can mean in your life. You are learning very early in life ways (which we did not know) of fighting an enemy, and also the value of unreserved trust in a friend. 'Has not man a hard service upon earth?' (Job 7.1.) 'Blessed be the Lord, my rock, who trains my hands for war, and my fingers for battle; my rock and my fortress, my stronghold and my deliverer, my shield and he in whom I take refuge' (Ps. 144.1f.). 'There is a friend who sticks closer than a brother' (Prov. 18.24).

Are we moving towards an age of colossal organization and

collective institutions, or will the desire of innumerable people for small, manageable, personal relationships be satisfied? Must they be mutually exclusive? Might it not be that world organizations themselves, with their wide meshes, will allow more scope for personal interests? Similarly with the question whether we are moving towards an age of the selection of the fittest, i.e. an aristocratic society, or to uniformity in all material and spiritual aspects of human life. Although there has been a very far-reaching equalization here, the sensitiveness in all ranks of society for the human values of justice, achievement, and courage could create a new selection of people who will be allowed the right to provide strong leadership. It will not be difficult for us to renounce our privileges, recognizing the justice of history. We may have to face events and changes that take no account of our wishes and our rights. But if so, we shall not give way to embittered and barren pride, but consciously submit to divine judgment, and so prove ourselves worthy to survive by identifying ourselves generously and unselfishly with the life of the community and the sufferings of our fellow-men. 'But any nation which will bring its neck under the yoke of the king of Babylon and serve him, I will leave on its own land, to till it and dwell there, says the Lord' (Jer. 27.11). 'Seek the welfare of the city . . . and pray to the Lord on its behalf' (Jer. 29.7). 'Come, my people, enter your chambers, and shut your doors behind you; hide yourselves for a little while until the wrath is past' (Isa. 26.20). 'For his anger is but for a moment, and his favour is for a lifetime. Weeping may tarry for the night, but joy comes with the morning' (Ps. 30.5).

Today you will be baptized a Christian. All those great ancient words of the Christian proclamation will be spoken over you, and the command of Jesus Christ to baptize will be carried out on you, without your knowing anything about it. But we are once again being driven right back to the beginnings of our understanding. Reconciliation and redemption, regeneration and the Holy Spirit, love of our enemies, cross and resurrection, life in Christ and Christian discipleship – all these things are so difficult and so remote that we hardly venture any more to speak of them. In the traditional words and acts we suspect that there may be something quite new and revolutionary, though we cannot as yet grasp or express it. That is our own fault. Our church, which has been fighting in these years only for its self-preservation, as though that were an end in itself, is incapable of taking the word of reconciliation and redemption to mankind and the world. Our earlier words are therefore bound to lose their force and cease, and our being Christians today will be limited to two things: prayer and righteous action among men. All Christian thinking, speaking, and organizing must be born anew out of this prayer and action. By the time you have grown up, the church's form will have changed greatly. We are not yet out of the melting-pot, and any attempt to help the church prematurely to a new expansion of its organization will merely delay its conversion and purification. It is not for us to prophesy the day (though the day will come) when men will once more be called so to utter the word of God that the world will be changed and renewed by it. It will be a new language, perhaps quite non-religious, but liberating and redeeming – as was Jesus' language; it will shock people and yet overcome them by its power; it will be the language of a new righteousness and truth, proclaiming God's peace with men and the coming of his kingdom. 'They shall fear and tremble because of all the good and all the prosperity I provide for it' (Jer. 33.9). Till then the Christian cause will be a silent and hidden affair, but there will be those who pray and do right and wait for God's own time. May you be one of them, and may it be said of you one day, 'The path of the righteous is like the light of dawn, which shines brighter and brighter till full day' (Prov. 4.18).

May 1944
Letters and Papers from Prison, 294–300

III · SUFFERING

Introduction

'Ambitious programmes always only take us where we are; but we should always find ourselves only where he is. Indeed we cannot be anywhere other than where he is. Or have I missed the place where he is? Where he is for me?' We read these words in the entry for 9 June 1939 in Bonhoeffer's diary of his trip to America, which more than any other document which he wrote gives us some insight into a process of decision which was probably the most momentous of his whole life. He had left Germany precisely because war was imminent. Ecumenical friends from the Western world had invited him to America in order to escape the fate of being entangled in Hitler's Reich, and had prepared a wealth of theological tasks and church work for him. He was barely two days out into the Atlantic when he began to have doubts whether he had made the right decision. These grew stronger day by day as he met friends and those in charge of his new duties in the USA. In the end he was convinced that he had to go back to Germany. One of the last entries in his diary reads: 'Perhaps I have learnt more in this month than in a whole year nine years ago; at least I have gained important insight for all future decisions. Probably this visit will have a great effect on me.'

What may he have learned? He had already known a great deal about the cross of Christ because he loved it, and also about discipleship, and that the cross was part of discipleship in his own land. Moreover, as early as January 1934 he had preached that sermon on Jeremiah 20.7, which can only be called prophetic, in which without being able to guess it, he anticipated the whole of his later life and especially his death. But now a new element had been added. He had to learn that one does not seek out the place of the presence of Christ where one would like it to be, that with the best will in the world it is possible to lose the way. Suddenly he knew that whatever else, he would not find Christ in the haven of ecumenical community in the United States. Discipleship summoned him back to solidarity with the Confessing Church which he had left behind in such great confusion, with his people and the guilt they had incurred, and above all on the side of those who in the midst of the outrages which were spreading over Germany would soon involve other nations in suffering, were resolved to set up a dam against chaos. There is a wealth of evidence that Bonhoeffer saw his urgent task in a wartime Germany as being this and not any other, and that he had no illusions about the danger and the suffering which he would meet on the way. Above all he saw that it was here that Christ was waiting for him, with completely new insights.

The wealth of these new insights can hardly be indicated now. But this wealth explains the fascination that the letters from prison have had all over the world down to the present day: the breadth of the Lordship of Christ which embraces areas which are traditionally thought to be removed from it; the unprejudiced analysis of a world becoming increasingly autonomous, increasingly religionless; consideration of the question how those who have become religionless can see in Jesus, the man for others, their brother, their liberator from many kinds of bonds; the deep this-worldliness of Christian faith; the description of being a Christian in terms of taking part in the action and suffering of God and Jesus Christ in the world. We find all this summed up in the most moving way in the letter which Bonhoeffer wrote on 21 July 1944, on the day after the failure of the attempt on Hitler's life, when he had to reckon with the probability of his imminent death. One of the last pages of this letter reads: 'I'm glad to have been able to learn this, and I know I've been able to do so only along the road that I've travelled. So I'm grateful for the past and present, and content with them.'

O.D.

Could we have known that your love causes so much pain?

Jer. 20.7: O Lord, you have persuaded me, and I am persuaded; you are stronger than I and you have prevailed.

Jeremiah did not push himself forward to become a prophet of God. He shrank back when the call suddenly reached him; he resisted, he wanted to avoid it – no, he did not want to be a prophet and witness of this God. But as he fled the Word, the call got him, grasped him; he could no longer escape, it had happened to him, God had his sacrifice, or as someone put it, the arrow of the almighty God hit the hunted deer. Jeremiah became his prophet.

It comes upon men and women from outside; it does not rise up from their heart's desires, from their most secret wishes and hopes. The word that challenges people, grasps them and holds them captive does not come from the depths of our souls but is the strange, unknown, unexpected, violent, overwhelming Word of the Lord who calls to his service whom he wills when he wills. It is no use struggling against it; we have God's reply: I knew you before I made you in your mother's womb; you are mine. Don't be afraid! I am your God, who holds you.

And then this alien, distant, unknown, violent word is all of a sudden the loving word of the Lord who longs for his creature – well known, uncannily near, persuasive, endearing, seductive. A lassoo is thrown over a man's head and he cannot get away; he finds it impossible to struggle against it, for the lassoo draws tighter and tighter and becomes more and more painful, to remind him that he is a prisoner. He is a prisoner and has to follow. The way is prescribed for him. It is the way of the man whom God will not let go, the man who will not let go of God; and that means that it is also the way of the man who will never again be God-less – in good times and in bad.

This way leads us into the depths of human weakness. This Jeremiah is a fool, ridiculed, despised, declared mad, but all the more of a threat to human peace and quiet; he is someone whom people beat, imprison, torture and would love to put to death immediately. And all this precisely because he can no longer be free of God. He has been accused of being a dreamer, a man with a bee in his bonnet, a disturber of the peace, an enemy of the people; that is the accusation that has always been levelled against those who have become possessed with and seized by God, for whom God has become too strong. How glad Jeremiah would have been to be able to speak differently; how glad he would have been to cry peace and salvation with the others, where there was unrest and disaster! How glad he would have been to be able to keep quiet, to acknowledge that others were right! But he simply could not: it was like a compulsion, a pressure on him; it was as though someone were riding on his shoulders, driving him from one truth to another, from one suffering to another. He was no longer his own master, he could no longer control himself; another had seized him, another possessed him, he was possessed by another. And Jeremiah was our flesh and blood, he was a man like we are. He suffered from the same permanent humiliations, mockery, violence, the brutality of others, and so after a painful torturing which had lasted all night, he burst out with this prayer: 'O Lord, you have persuaded me, and I am persuaded; you are stronger than I, and you have prevailed.'

My God, you have done the same thing to me. You have lain in wait for me, you have not wanted to let me go, you have always tended suddenly to get in my way here and there, you have seduced and charmed me, you have made my heart compliant and willing, you have spoken to me of your longing and eternal love, your fidelity and strength; when I sought power, you strengthened me; when I sought support, you held me up; when I sought forgiveness, you forgave me my guilt. I did not want it, but you overcame my will, my resistance, my heart; my God, you irresistibly seduced me so that I yielded to you. Lord, you have persuaded me and I am persuaded. You caught me unsuspecting – and now I cannot be away from you, now you haul me away as your booty, you bind us to your chariot and drag us behind you, so that we join in your triumphal procession shamed and tortured. Could we have known that your love causes so much pain, that your grace is so hard? You have become too strong for me and you have won. When the thought of you became strong in me, I became weak. When you prevailed over me, I was lost; my will was broken, my strength was too little. I had to go the way of suffering; I could no longer resist you, I could not go back; the decision over my life was taken. I did not decide, but you did. You have bound me to you, for better or worse. O God, why are you so terribly near to us?

Not to be able to get away from God is the disturbing restriction on any Christian life. Anyone who accepts it, who allows themselves to be persuaded by God, cannot get away, just as a child cannot get away from its mother or a husband from the wife whom he loved. Anyone to whom God has once spoken can never again completely forget him; God continues to go with him, in good or ill; God follows a man, like his shadow. And this enduring nearness of God becomes too much for a man, too big; it is stronger than he, and he may well think, 'If only I had never encountered God! It is too hard for me, it destroys my peace of mind and my happiness.' But that is no longer any use. He cannot get away; and now he must go through with it, go with God, come what may. And though he may think that he can no longer bear it, that he must make an end of himself, he also knows that even if he does that he will not get away from the God in whom he trusts, by whom he has allowed himself to be overcome; he remains God's victim, in his hands.

But precisely at this point, where someone thinks that he can no longer continue on the way with God because it is too difficult – and such hours come to everyone at some time – where God has become too strong for us – where a Christian collapses under God and fails – there God's nearness, God's faithfulness, God's strength becomes a comfort and a help; for only then do we recognize God and the significance of our Christian life aright. No longer to be able to get away from God means much anxiety, much despondency, much tribulation, but it also means never being able to be God-less, in good times and in bad. It means God with us on all our ways, in faith and in sin, in persecution, mockery and death. What do we matter; our life, our happiness, our peace, our weakness, our sin, provided that the word, the will and the Power of God are glorified in our weak, mortal, sinful life, that our weakness becomes a vessel of the divine power. Prisoners do not wear proud garments, but chains. However, these chains glorify the one who goes victoriously through the world and mankind. Our chains and the tattered clothes that we must wear are in praise of him who glorifies truth and love and grace in us. The victorious procession of truth and righteousness, the trumphal procession of God and his gospel through this world drag behind the victor's chariot the bound and the prisoners.

May he finally bind us behind his chariot, so that though bound and disgraced we may take part in his victory! He has persuaded us that he has become too strong for us, and will never let us go. What do we care about chains and wounds, what do we care about sin and suffering and death? He holds us fast. He will not let us go. Lord, always persuade us anew and overpower us, that we may believe, live and die only in you, and see your victory.

21 January 1934
Predigten I, 425–30

The beatitudes

'*Blessed are the poor in spirit, for theirs is the kingdom of heaven.*' Privation is the lot of the disciples in every sphere of their lives. They are the 'poor' *tout court* (Luke 6.20). They have no security, no possessions to call their own, not even a foot of earth to call their home, no earthly society to claim their absolute allegiance. Nay more, they have no spiritual power, experience or knowledge to afford them consolation or security. For his sake they have lost all. In following him they lost even their own selves, and everything that could make them rich. Now they are poor – so inexperienced, so stupid, that they have no other hope but him who called them. Jesus knows all about the others too, the representatives and preachers of the national religion, who enjoy greatness and renown, whose feet are firmly planted on the earth, who are deeply rooted in the culture and piety of the people and moulded by the spirit of the age. Yet it is not they, but the disciples who are called blessed – *theirs* is the kingdom of heaven. That kingdom dawns on *them*, the little band who for the sake of Jesus live a life of absolute renunciation and poverty. And in that very poverty they are heirs of the kingdom. They have their treasure in secret, they find it on the cross. And they have the promise that they will one day visibly enjoy the glory of the kingdom, which in principle is already realized in the utter poverty of the cross.

This beatitude is poles removed from the caricatures of it which appear in political and social manifestos. The Antichrist also calls the poor blessed, but not for the sake of the cross, which embraces all poverty and transforms it into a source of blessing. He fights the cross with political and sociological ideology. He may call it Christian, but that only makes him a still more dangerous enemy.

'Blessed are they that mourn, for they shall be comforted.' With each beatitude the gulf is widened between the disciples and the people, their call to come forth from the people becomes increasingly manifest. By 'mourning' Jesus, of course, means doing without what the world calls peace and prosperity: He means refusing to be in tune with the world or to accommodate oneself to its standards. Such men mourn for the world, for its guilt, its fate and its fortune. While the world keeps holiday they stand aside, and while the world sings, 'Gather ye rose-buds while ye may', they mourn. They see that for all the jollity on board, the ship is beginning to sink. The world dreams of progress, of power and of the future, but the disciples meditate on the end, the last judgment, and the coming of the kingdom. To such heights the world cannot rise. And so the disciples are strangers in the world, unwelcome guests and disturbers of the peace. No wonder the world rejects them! Why does the Christian church so often have to look on from outside when the nation is celebrating? Have churchmen no understanding and sympathy for their fellow-men? Have they become victims of misanthropy? Nobody loves his fellow-men better than a disciple, nobody understands his fellow-men better than the Christian fellowship, and that very love impels them to stand aside and mourn. It was a happy and suggestive thought of Luther, to translate the Greek word here by the German *Leidtragen* (sorrow-bearing). For the emphasis lies on the *bearing* of sorrow. The disciple-community does not shake off sorrow as though it were no concern of its own, but willingly bears it. And in this way they show how close are the bonds which bind them to the rest of humanity. But at the same time they do not go out of their way to look for suffering, or try to contract out of it by adopting an attitude of contempt and disdain. They simply bear the suffering which comes their way as they try to follow Jesus Christ, and bear it for *his* sake. Sorrow cannot tire them or wear them down, it cannot embitter them or cause them to break down under the strain; far from it, for they bear their sorrow in the strength of him who bears them up, who bore the whole suffering

99

of the world upon the cross. They stand as the bearers of sorrow in the fellowship of the Crucified: they stand as strangers in the world in the power of him who was such a stranger to the world that it crucified him. This is their comfort, or better still, this *man* is their comfort, the Comforter (cf. Luke 2.25). The community of strangers find their comfort in the cross, they are comforted by being cast upon the place where the Comforter of Israel awaits them. Thus do they find their true home with their crucified Lord, both here and in eternity.

'Blessed are the meek: for they shall inherit the earth.' This community of strangers possesses no inherent right of its own to protect its members in the world, nor do they claim such rights, for they are meek, they renounce every right of their own and live for the sake of Jesus Christ. When reproached, they hold their peace; when treated with violence they endure it patiently; when men drive them from their presence, they yield their ground. They will not go to law to defend their rights, or make a scene when they suffer injustice, nor do they insist on their legal rights. They are determined to leave their rights to God alone – *non cupidi vindictae*, as the ancient church paraphrased it. Their right is in the will of their lord – that and no more. They show by every word and gesture that they do not belong to this earth. Leave heaven to them, says the world in its pity, that is where they belong. But Jesus says: 'They shall inherit the earth.' To these, the powerless and the disenfranchised, the very earth belongs. Those who now possess it by violence and injustice shall lose it, and those who here have utterly renounced it, who were meek to the point of the cross, shall rule the new earth. We must not interpret this as a reference to God's exercise of juridical punishment within the world, as Calvin did: what it means is that when the kingdom of heaven descends, the face of the earth will be renewed, and it will belong to the flock of Jesus. God does not forsake the earth: he made it, he sent his Son to it, and on it he built his church. Thus a beginning has already been made in this present age. A sign has been given. The powerless have here and now received a plot of earth, for they have the church and its fellowship, its goods, its brothers and sisters, in the midst of persecutions even to the length of the cross. The renewal of the earth begins at Golgotha,

where the meek one died, and from thence it will spread. When the kingdom finally comes, the meek shall possess the earth.

'*Blessed are they that hunger and thirst after righteousness: for they shall be filled.*' Not only do the followers of Jesus renounce their rights, they *renounce their own righteousness* too. They get no praise for their achievements or sacrifices. They cannot have righteousness except by hungering and thirsting for it (this applies equally to their own righteousness and to the righteousness of God on earth), always they look forward to the future righteousness of God, but they cannot establish it for themselves. Those who follow Jesus grow hungry and thirsty on the way. They are longing for the forgiveness of all sin, for complete renewal, for the renewal too of the earth and the full establishment of God's law. They are still involved in the world's curse, and affected by its sin. He whom they follow must die accursed on the cross, with a desperate cry for righteousness on his lips: 'My God, my God, why hast thou forsaken me?' But the disciple is not above his master, he follows in his steps. Happy are they who have the promise that they shall be filled, for the righteousness they receive will be no empty promise, but real satisfaction. They will eat the Bread of Life in the Messianic Feast. They are blessed because they already enjoy this bread here and now, for in their hunger they are sustained by the bread of life, the bliss of sinners.

'*Blessed are the merciful, for they shall obtain mercy.*' These men without possessions of power, these strangers on earth, these sinners, these followers of Jesus, have in their life with him *renounced their own dignity*, for they are merciful. As if their own needs and their own distress were not enough, they take upon themselves the distress and humiliation and sin of others. They have an irresistible love for the down-trodden, the sick, the wretched, the wronged, the outcast and all who are tortured with anxiety. They go out and seek all who are enmeshed in the toils of sin and guilt. No distress is too great, no sin too appalling for their pity. If any man falls into disgrace, the merciful will sacrifice their own honour to shield him, and take his shame upon themselves. They will be found consorting with publicans and sinners, careless of the shame they incur thereby. In order that they may be merciful they cast away the most priceless treasure of human life, their personal dignity and honour. For the only honour and dignity they know is their Lord's own mercy, to which alone they owe their very lives. He was not ashamed of his disciples, he became the brother of mankind, and bore their shame unto the death of the cross. That is how Jesus, the crucified, was merciful. His followers owe their lives entirely to that mercy. It makes them forget their own honour and dignity, and seek the society of sinners. They are glad to incur reproach, for they know that then they are blessed. One day God himself will come down and take upon himself their sin and shame. He will cover them with his own honour and remove their disgrace. It will be his glory to bear the shame of sinners and to clothe them with his honour. Blessed are the merciful, for they have the Merciful for their Lord.

'*Blessed are the pure in heart: for they shall see God.*' Who is pure in heart? Only those who have surrendered their hearts completely to Jesus that he may reign in them alone. Only those whose hearts are undefiled by their own evil – and by their own virtues too. The pure in heart have a child-like simplicity like Adam before the fall, innocent alike of good and evil: their hearts are not ruled by their conscience, but by the will of Jesus. If men renounce their own good, if in penitence they have renounced their own hearts, if they rely solely upon Jesus, then his word purifies their hearts. Purity of heart is here contrasted with all outward purity, even the purity of high intentions. The pure heart is pure alike of good and evil, it belongs exclusively to Christ and looks only to him who goes on before. Only they will see God, who in this life have looked solely unto Jesus Christ, the Son of God. For them their hearts are free from all defiling phantasies and are not distracted by conflicting desires and intentions. They are wholly absorbed by the contemplation of God. They shall see God, whose hearts have become a reflection of the image of Jesus Christ.

'*Blessed are the peacemakers: for they shall be called the children of God.*' The followers of Jesus have been called to peace. When he called them they found their peace, for he is their peace. But now they are told that they must not only *have* peace but *make* it. And to that end they renounce all violence and tumult. In the cause of Christ nothing is to be gained by such methods. His kingdom is one of peace, and the mutual greeting of his flock is a greeting of peace. His disciples keep the peace by choosing to endure suffering themselves rather than inflict it on others. They maintain fellowship where others would break it off. They renounce all self-assertion, and quietly suffer in the face of hatred and wrong. In so doing they overcome evil with good, and establish the peace of God in the midst of a world of war and hate. But nowhere will that peace be more manifest than where they meet the wicked in peace and are ready to suffer at their hands. The peacemakers will carry the cross with their Lord, for it was on the cross that peace was made. Now that they are partners in Christ's work of reconciliation, they are called the sons of God as he is the Son of God.

'Blessed are they that have been persecuted for righteousness' sake: for theirs is the kingdom of heaven.' This does not refer to the righteousness of God, but to suffering in a just cause, suffering for their own just judgments and actions. For it is by these that they who renounce possessions, fortune, rights, righteousness, honour, and force for the sake of following Christ, will be distinguished from the world. The world will be offended at them, and so the disciples will be persecuted for righteousness' sake. Not recognition, but rejection, is the reward they get from the world for their message and works. It is important that Jesus gives his blessing not merely to suffering incurred directly for the confession of his name, but to suffering in any just cause. They receive the same promise as the poor, for in persecution they are their equals in poverty.

Having reached the end of the beatitudes, we naturally ask if there is any place on this earth for the community which they describe. Clearly, there is one place, and only one, and that is where the poorest, meekest, and most sorely tried of all men is to be found – on the cross of Golgotha. The fellowship of the beatitudes is the fellowship of the Crucified. With him it has lost all, and with him it has found all. From the cross there comes the call 'blessed, blessed'. The last beatitude is addressed directly to the disciples, for only they can understand it, 'Blessed are ye when men shall reproach you, and persecute you, and say all manner of evil against you falsely for my sake. Rejoice and be exceeding glad, for great is your reward in heaven: for so persecuted they the prophets which were before you.' 'For my sake' the disciples are reproached, but because it is for his sake, the reproach falls on him. It is he who bears the guilt. The curse, the deadly persecution and evil slander confirm the blessed state of the disciples in their fellowship with Jesus. It could not be otherwise, for these meek strangers are bound to provoke the world to insult, violence and slander. Too menacing, too loud are the voices of these poor meek men, too patient and too silent their suffering. Too powerful are the testimony of their poverty and their endurance of the wrongs of the world. This is fatal, and so, while Jesus calls them blessed, the world cries: 'Away with them, away with them!' Yes, but whither? To the kingdom of heaven. 'Rejoice and be exceeding glad: for great is your reward in heaven.' There shall the poor be seen in the halls of joy. With his own hand God wipes away the tears from the eyes of those who had mourned upon earth. He feeds the hungry at his Banquet. There stand the scarred bodies of the martyrs, now glorified and clothed in the white robes of eternal righteousness instead of the rags of sin and repentance. The echoes of this joy reach the little flock below as it stands beneath the cross, and they hear Jesus saying: 'Blessed are ye!'

The Cost of Discipleship, 97–103

Discipleship and the cross

'If any man would come after me, let him deny himself.' The disciple must say to himself the same words Peter said of Christ when he denied him: 'I know not this man.' Self-denial is never just a series of isolated acts of mortification or asceticism. It is not suicide, for there is an element of self-will even in that. To deny oneself is to be aware only of Christ and no more of self, to see only him who goes before and no more the road which is too hard for us. Once more, all that self-denial can say is: 'He leads the way, keep close to him.'

Suffering has to be endured in order that it may pass away. Either the world must bear the whole burden and collapse beneath it, or it must fall on Christ to be overcome in him. He therefore suffers vicariously for the world. His is the only suffering which has redemptive efficacy. But the church knows that the world is still seeking for someone to bear its sufferings, and so, as it follows Christ, suffering becomes the church's lot too and bearing it, it is borne up by Christ. As it follows him beneath the cross, the church stands before God as the representative of the world.

For God is a God who *bears*. The Son of God bore our flesh, he bore the cross, he bore our sins, thus making atonement for us. In the same way his followers are also called upon to bear, and that is precisely what it means to be a Christian. Just as Christ maintained his communion with the Father by his endurance, so his followers are to maintain their communion with Christ by their endurance. We can of course shake off the burden which is laid upon us, but only find that we have a still heavier burden to carry – a yoke of our own choosing, the yoke of our self. But Jesus invites all who travail and are heavy laden to throw off their own yoke and take his yoke upon them–and his yoke is easy, and his burden is light. The yoke and the burden of Christ are his cross. To go one's way under the sign of the cross is not misery and desperation, but peace and refreshment for the soul, it is the highest joy. Then we do not walk under our self-made laws and burdens, but under the yoke of him who knows us and who walks under the yoke with us. Under his yoke we are certain of his nearness and communion. It is he whom the disciple finds as he lifts up his cross.

'Discipleship is not limited to what you can comprehend – it must transcend all comprehension. Plunge into the deep waters beyond your own comprehension, and I will help you to comprehend even as I do. Bewilderment is the true comprehension. Not to know where you are going is the true knowledge. My comprehension transcends yours. Thus Abraham went forth from his father and not knowing whither he went. He trusted himself to my knowledge, and cared not for his own, and thus he took the right road and came to his journey's end. Behold, that is the way of the cross. You cannot find it yourself, so you must let me lead you as though you were a blind man. Wherefore it is not you, no man, no living creature, but I myself, who instruct you by my word and Spirit in the way you should go. Not the work which you choose, not the suffering you devise, but the road which is clean contrary to all that you choose or contrive or desire – that is the road you must take. To that I call you and in that you must be my disciple. If you do that, there is the acceptable time and there your master is come' (Luther).

The Cost of Discipleship, 77f., 81ff.

From the diary of the American trip

Zech 7.9: Render true judgment, show kindness and mercy each to his brother.

Matt. 5.7: Blessed are the merciful, for they shall receive mercy.

'Render true judgment . . .' That is my first request to you, brothers at home. I do not want to be spared in your thoughts. But what can judgment before the merciful God, before the cross of Christ be, if not merciful? No blind mercy, for that would not be merciful; but a clear-sighted, forgiving, brotherly mercy as true judgment on us.

'Render true judgment . . .' That is a necessary warning and instruction for the task in America. It rules out any high spirits and makes the task a serious one. To see others as brothers under the mercy of Jesus Christ and no longer to speak from one's own particular knowledge or experience, we must be merciful; we cannot be jesuitical. May God continue to have mercy on us!

9 June 1939

Isa. 41.9: You shall be my servant; for I have chosen you and will not reject you

John 12.26: If any one serves me, he must follow me; and where I am, there shall my servant be also.

God chooses the sinner to be his servant, so that his grace may become quite clear. The sinner is to do his work and extend his grace. God gives work to those whom he has forgiven. But this service can consist only in discipleship. Great programmes always take us only where we ourselves are; but we should only allow ourselves to be found where he is. Indeed we cannot be anywhere other than where he is. Whether you are working over there or I am working in America, we are both only where he is. He takes us with him. Or have I missed the place where he is? Where he is for me? No. God says, 'You are my servant.'

10 June 1939

Ps. 28.7: The Lord is my strength and my shield; in him my

106

heart trusts; so I am helped and my heart exults, and with
my song I give thanks to him.

Eph. 4.30: And do not grieve the Holy Spirit of God, in whom
you were sealed for the day of redemption.

In what can 'the heart exult' other than in the daily certainty that
God is our dear Father and Jesus Christ our saviour? With what
can we grieve the Holy Spirit more than if we cling to sorrowful
thoughts and do not entrust ourselves confidently to his guidance,
his words, his comfort? Until the day of deliverance comes, finally
comes!

11 June 1939

Ps. 44.21: For he knows the secrets of the heart.

I Cor. 13.12: For now we see in a mirror dimly; but then face
to face.

Today is Sunday. No service. Moreover the hours have already
changed so much that I can no longer share in your service at the
time you have it. But I am utterly with you, today more than ever.
If only I could get over my doubts about what I am doing. One's
own searching for the secrets of the heart, which are unfathomable.
'He knows the secrets of the heart.' When the mixture of accu-
sations and excuses, desires and anxieties make everything in us
obscure, he sees clearly to our very depths. But there he finds a
name which he himself has inscribed: Jesus Christ. That's how we
are to celebrate Sunday. One day we shall know and see what we
now believe; one day we shall hold a service together in eternity.

> Beginning and end, Lord, are thine,
> the life lived between them was mine.
> Though lost and in darkness I happen to roam,
> With thee, Lord, is brightness, and light is thy home.
>
> Just a while longer, then all will be done,
> then the whole battle its course will have run.
> Then may I drink of live's living spring,
> And converse for ever with Jesus, my king.
> (Epitaphs of Fritz Reuter and Søren Kierkegaard)

Deut. 6.6: And these words which I command you this day shall be upon your heart . . .

Acts 15.40: Paul departed, being commended by the brethren to the grace of the Lord.

'Paul departed, being commended by the brethren to the grace of the Lord.' Arrival in New York. It was crucial to know in these first hours that the brethren have commended us to the grace of the Lord.

Gesammelte Schriften I, 291–295

13 June 1939

Breakfast with Leiper, who greeted me most kindly and fetched me. First discussion of the future. I am taking as the firm starting point for everything that I want to go back in a year at the latest. Astonishment. But I am quite clear that I must go back . . .

The country house in Lakeville, Connecticut is in the hills; fresh and luxuriant vegetation. In the evening thousands of fire-flies in the garden, flying glow-worms. I had never seen them before. Quite a fantastic sight. Very friendly and 'informal' reception. All I need is Germany, the brethren. The first lonely hours are hard. I do not understand why I am here, whether it was a sensible thing to do, whether the results will be worthwhile. In the evening, last of all, the readings and thoughts about work at home. I have now been almost two weeks without knowing what is going on there. It is hard to bear. 'It is good that one should wait quietly for the salvation of the Lord' (Lam. 3.26).

14 June 1939

Breakfast on the veranda at eight. It poured in the night. Everything is fresh and clean. Then prayers. I was almost overcome by the short prayer – the whole family knelt down – in which we thought of the German brethren . . .

15 June 1939

Since yesterday evening I haven't been able to stop thinking of Germany. I would not have thought it possible that at my age, after so many years abroad, one could get so dreadfully homesick.

What was in itself a wonderful motor expedition this morning to a female acquaintance in the country, i.e., in the hills, became almost unbearable. We sat for an hour and chattered, not in a silly way, true, but about things which left me completely cold – whether it is possible to get a good musical education in New York, about the education of children, etc., etc., and I thought how usefully I could be spending these hours in Germany. I would gladly have taken the next ship home. This inactivity, or rather activity in unimportant things, is quite intolerable when one thinks of the brethren and of how precious time is. The whole burden of self-reproach because of a wrong decision comes back again and almost overwhelms one. I was in utter despair. In the afternoon I tried to do some work. Then I was invited for a second trip into the hills of Massachusetts. It was at quite the wrong time. I still hadn't found peace for Bible reading and prayer. The trip was splendid. We went through a whole stretch of laurel wood. The view from above was rather like the Harz country. But the burden did not leave me all day . . . How glad I was to begin the readings again in the evening and find 'My heart shall rejoice in thy salvation' (Ps. 13.5).

16 June 1939

A fortnight ago today I left Berlin and already I long so much for work. Return to New York. Evening at last. I needed it badly. One is less lonely when one is alone . . .

I am waiting for the post! It is almost unbearable. Probably I shall not have to wait long. Today God's Word says, 'I am coming soon' (Rev. 3.11). There is no time to lose, and here I am wasting days, perhaps weeks. In any case, it seems like that at the moment. Then I say to myself again, 'It is cowardice and weakness to run away here now.' Will I ever be able to do any really significant work here? – Disquieting political news from Japan. If it becomes unsettled now I am definitely going back to Germany. I cannot stay outside by myself. That is quite clear. My whole life is still over there.

Spent the whole day in the library, looking through *The Christian Century*. Instructive articles on 'How my mind has changed in the last decade'. Professors of theology on the change in American theology since 1929. The decisive shift to the Word still does not seem to have been made; instead, the movement seems to be from a belief in progress to nihilism, from ethicism to a philosophy to the 'present', the 'concrete situation'. Account of the last lynching of a Negro. Two white people go into the house and pray with the Negroes that 'the day may come when such things will not happen in America'. That is a good solution for such happenings. Also a report on the lack of religion among college students – 'disinterested'. That must happen if one doesn't eventually realize that 'religion' is really superfluous.

Sunday 18 June 1939

How good the readings are today! Ps. 119, 105; Matt. 13.8. Work in the afternoon. Spoke to no one all day. Now I must begin to learn again how fortunate I have been hitherto always to have been in the company of the brethren. And Niemöller has been alone for two years. To imagine it! What a faith, what a discipline, and what a clear act of God! – Now the day has had a good ending. I went to church again. As long as there are lonely Christians there will always be services. It is a great help after a couple of quite lonely days to go into church and there pray together, sing together, listen together. The sermon was astonishing (Broadway Presbyterian Church, Dr McComb) on 'our likeness with Christ'. A completely biblical sermon – the sections on 'we are *blameless* like Christ', 'we are *tempted* like Christ' were particularly good. This will one day be a centre of resistance when Riverside Church has long since become a temple of Baal. I was very glad about this sermon. Why does a man who preaches like that not notice what dreadful music he has played? I will ask him. This sermon opened up to me an America of which I was quite ignorant before. Otherwise I would have become quite ungrateful in these days for all the protection which God has given me. With my intention and inner need to think incessantly of the brethren over there and their work I would almost have avoided the task here. It began to seem treacherous not to have all my thoughts over there. I still have to find the right balance. Paul writes that he thinks of his congregation 'without ceasing' in his prayers and yet at the same time he devoted himself completely to the task in hand. I must learn to do that. It will probably only come with prayer. God, grant me in the next few weeks clarity about my future and keep me in the communion of prayer with the brethren.

Without news from Germany the whole day, from post to post, waiting in vain. It does not help to get angry and write that sort of letter. The expected news is there long before the letter arrives. I want to know how work is going over there, whether all is well or whether they need me. I want to have some sign from over there before the decisive meeting tomorrow. Perhaps it is a good thing that it has not come. The news about China is disquieting. Will one be able to get home in time if it gets serious? – Spent the whole day in the library. Wrote English lectures. I have great difficulty with the language. They say that I speak English well, and yet I find it so utterly inadequate. How many years, how many decades has it taken to learn German, and even now one does not know it! I will never learn English. That is already one reason for going back home soon. Without language one is lost, hopelessly lonely. In the evening to Times Square, an escape. News-reel there for an hour. Early to bed. What a day! But: 'The name of the Lord Jesus was extolled' (Acts 19.17). It disturbs me that we do not keep the same time as Germany. It hinders and prevents prayer together. It is the same every evening. But: 'We thank thee, O God . . . that thy name is so near' (Ps. 75.1).

In the morning a letter from my parents from South Germany. Nothing from Stettin. Visit Leiper. The decision has been made. I have refused. They were clearly disappointed, and rather upset. It probably means more for me than I can see at the moment. God alone knows what. It is remarkable how I am never quite clear about the motives for any of my decisions. Is that a sign of confusion, of inner dishonesty, or is it a sign that we are guided without our knowing, or is it both?

Isa. 45.19; I Peter 1.17.

Today the reading speaks dreadfully harshly of God's incorruptible judgment. He certainly sees how much personal feeling, how much anxiety there is in today's decision, however brave it may seem. The reasons one gives for an action to others and to one's self are certainly inadequate. One can give a reason for everything. In the last resort one acts from a level which remains hidden from us. So one can only ask God to judge us and to forgive us.

Of course I still keep having second thoughts about my decision. One could have also given quite different reasons; first, I am here (and perhaps the very misunderstanding was a guidance); they say that it was like the answer to a prayer when my coming was announced; they would like to have *me*; they cannot understand why I refuse; it upsets all their plans for the future; I have no news from home and perhaps everything is going well without me, etc. Or one could ask: have I simply acted out of a longing for Germany and the work there? And is this almost incomprehensible and hitherto almost completely unknown homesickness an accompanying sign from above to make refusal easier for me? Or, is it not irresponsible towards so many other men simply to say *no* to one's own future and that of many others? Will I regret it? I may not. Desite everything there is first of all the promise, then the joy of working at home and finally the other, that I am trying to suppress. The reading is again so harsh: 'He will sit as a refiner of gold and silver' (Mal. 3.3). And it is necessary. I don't know where I am. But he knows; and in the end all doings and actions will be pure and clear.

The evening papers bring very excited news about Japan. Bewer calms me down. It is unbearable over here for a German; one is simply torn in two. Whereas a catastrophe here is quite inconceivable, unless it is ordained. But even to be responsible, to have to reproach oneself, for having come out unnecessarily, is certainly crushing. But we cannot part ourselves from our destiny, much less here, outside; here everything lies solely on one's own shoulders, and one has no voice and no rights in a foreign land. Besides, the storm will also soon break here, too. It is already bubbling fiercely under the surface. And woe betide those who are aliens here. It is strange how strongly I have been moved by these particular thoughts in the last few days and how all thoughts about the *Una Sancta* make slow progress. A tremendous amount has already been overwhelmed. I have been writing in bed since yesterday evening. A good ending. All that remains now is the readings and intercessions. In the morning a discussion with Bewer and Van Dusen about the future. I want to go back in August. They urge me to stay longer. But if nothing happens in the meantime I shall stick by 12 August . . .

24 June 1939

Post at last. That is a great relief. But once again it is quite clear that I must go back to work. I have done quite a lot today. W. A. Brown, 'State and Church', etc. Rodewell held me up too long in the morning. I now often wonder whether it is true that America is the country without a reformation. If reformation means the God-given knowledge of the failure of all ways of building up a kingdom of God on earth, then it is probably true. But is it not also true of England? The voice of Lutheranism is there in America, but it is one among others: it has never been able to confront the other denominations. There hardly ever seem to be 'encounters' in this great country, in which the one can always avoid the other. But where there is no encounter, where liberty is the only unifying factor, one naturally knows nothing of the community which is created through encounter. The whole life together is completely different as a result. Community in our sense, whether cultural or ecclesiastical, cannot develop there. Is that true? – Wrote cards in the evening. Felix Gilbert called. – The newspapers are grim again today. Readings: 'The one who believes does not flee' (Isa. 28.16). I'm thinking of work at home. Tomorrow is Sunday. I wonder if I shall hear a *sermon*?

26 June 1939

Today, by chance, I read II Tim. 4.21, 'Do your best to come before winter' – Paul's request to Timothy. Timothy is to share the suffering of the apostle and not to be ashamed. 'Do your best to come before winter' – otherwise it might be too late. That has been in my ears all day. We are just like soldiers who come away from the field on leave and despite everything that they expected are forced back there again. We cannot get away from it. Not as though we were necessary, as though we were needed (by God?!), but simply because our life is there and because we leave our life behind, we destroy it, if we are not back there. There is nothing pious about it, but something almost vital. But God acts not only through pious emotions, but also through these vital ones. 'Do your best to come before winter' – It is not a misuse of scripture if I take that to be said to *me*. If God gives me grace to do it.

27 June 1939

Letter from my parents. Great joy, quite surprising. Work lunch-time and afternoon in the library. Tillich, Niebuhr. In the evening a visit from Professor Richardson, long conversation. He is an Englishman. One seems to stand nearer to him than to the Americans. I wonder if the Americans do not understand us at all because they are people who left Europe so as to be able to live out their faith for themselves in freedom? i.e. because they did not stand fast by the last decision in the question of belief? I feel that they would understand the fugitive better than the one who stays. Hence the American tolerance, or rather, indifference in dogmatic questions. A warlike encounter is excluded, but so too is the true passionate longing for unity in faith.

28 June 1939

The newspaper reports get more and more disturbing. They distract one's thoughts. I cannot imagine that it is God's will for me to remain here without anything particular to do in case of war. I must travel at the first possible opportunity.

29 June 1939

The news today is so bad that I am determined to go back with Karl Friedrich. We will discuss it tomorrow. Roberts spoke very critically about the church in America. The need comes from inside. Complete indifference towards its message continually dissolves the church. 'Keep away from politics' – says that the church should limit itself to its 'religious task', in which no one is interested. I find it more and more difficult to understand how the principle of a separation of church and state fits in with the practice of the social, economic, organizational and political activity of the church. In any case, the separation of church and state does not result in the church continuing to apply itself to its own task; it is no guarantee against secularization. Nowhere is the

114

church more secularized than where it is separated in principle as it is here. This very separation can create an opposition, so that the church engages much more strongly in political and secular things. That is probably important for our decisions over there.

1 July 1939

Went round in the morning. Karl Friedrich at mid-day. Wrote a bit in the afternoon. Then with K. F. into town, bought presents, Music Hall, cinema, the largest. Dreadful. Gaudy, ostentatious, vulgar colours, music and flesh. One can only find this sort of fantasy in a big city. K.F. disagrees. Home in good time in the evening. I could not get away all day from thinking about the situation in Germany and in the church. The readings are again very good. Job 41.11, 'God says, Who has given to me, that I should repay him? Whatever is under the whole heaven is mine.' Rom. 11.36: 'By him and through him and to him are all things. To him be glory for ever. Amen.' The earth, nations, Germany, and above all, the church, cannot fall from his hand. It was dreadfully hard for me to think and to pray 'Thy will be done' in view of the present situation. But it must be. Tomorrow is Sunday. May God make his Word find a hearing in all the world.

Sunday 2 July 1939

The Americans speak so much about freedom in their sermons. Freedom as a possession is a doubtful thing for a church; freedom must be won under the compulsion of a necessity. Freedom for the church comes from the necessity of the Word of God. Otherwise it becomes arbitrariness and ends in a great many new ties. Whether the church in America is really 'free', I doubt. They are lonely Sundays over here. Only the Word makes a true community. I need some good communal prayers in my own language. The news is not good. Will we arrive in time? Reading: Isa. 35.10! Intercessions.

6 July 1939

I'm writing on the ship. The last two days were so full that I did not get to writing. – In the morning down town to finalize travel arrangements. On the way back the Stock Exchange. Shopping. About 2.30 p.m. I met Paul Lehmann in my room; he had come from Columbus Ohio to see me again. Great delight. From now on I shall be spending the rest of the time with him. Prepared lecture.

7 July 1939

Last day. Paul tried to keep me back. It's no good. Van Dusen lecture. Pack. With Hans Wedell before lunch. Theological conversation with Paul. Farewell in the seminary. Supper with Van Dusen. Go to the ship with Paul. Farewell half past eleven, sail at half past twelve. Manhattan by night; the moon over the skyscrapers. It is very hot. The visit is at an end. I am glad to have been over and glad that I am on the way home. Perhaps I have learnt more in this month than in a whole year nine years ago; at least I have acquired some important insight for all future decisions. Probably this visit will have a great effect on me.

9 July 1939

English service, which was well attended, but probably as a change from the monotonous life on board, like the cinema etc. Text: 'There will be no more sea' (Rev. 21.1). Sermon sentimental and wordy. Conversation with Karl Friedrich about theological matters. Read a great deal. The days are noticeably shorter by the loss of an hour. Since I have been on the ship my inner uncertainty about the future has ceased. I can think of my shortened time in America without reproaches. Reading: 'It is good fo me that I was afflicted, that I might learn thy statues' (Ps. 119.71). One of my favourite verses from my favourite psalm.

The Way to Freedom, 227–247
Gesammelte Schriften I, 296–315

Lost years?

I heard someone say yesterday that the last years had been completely wasted as far as he was concerned. I'm very glad that I have never yet had that feeling, even for a moment. Nor have I ever regretted my decision in the summer of 1939, for I'm firmly convinced – however strange it may seem – that my life has followed a straight and unbroken course, at any rate in its outward conduct. It has been an uninterrupted enrichment of experience, for which I can only be thankful. If I were to end my life here in these conditions, that would have a meaning that I think I could understand; on the other hand, everything might be a thorough preparation for a new start and a new task when peace comes.

11 April 1944

Letters and Papers from Prison, 272

Protected from getting blunt

Some of us suffer a great deal from having our senses dulled in the face of all the sorrows which these war years have brought with them. Someone said to me recently, 'I pray every day for my senses not to become dulled.' That is certainly a good prayer. And yet we must be careful not to confuse ourselves with Christ. Christ endured all suffering and all human guilt to the full. Indeed he was Christ in that he suffered everything alone. But Christ could suffer alongside men because at the same time he was able to redeem them from suffering. He had his power to suffer with men from his love and his power to redeem men. We are not called to burden ourselves with the sorrows of the whole world; in the end, we cannot suffer with men in our own strength because we are unable to redeem. A suppressed desire to suffer with man in one's own strength must become resignation. We are simply called to look with utter joy on the one who really suffered with men and became their redeemer. We may joyfully believe that there was, there is, a man to whom no human sorrow and no human sin is strange and who in the profoundest love achieved our redemption. Only in such joy towards Christ, the Redeemer, are we saved from having our senses dulled by the pressure of human sorrow, or from becoming resigned under the experience of suffering.

True Patriotism, 189f.

Participation in the fate of Germany

Now I want to assure you that I haven't for a moment regretted coming back in 1939 – nor any of the consequences, either. I knew quite well what I was doing, and I acted with a clear conscience. I've no wish to cross out of my life anything that has happened since, either to me personally (would I have got engaged otherwise? would you have married? Sigurdshof, East Prussia, Ettal, my illness and all the help you gave me then, and the time in Berlin), or as regards events in general. And I regard my being kept here (do you remember that I prophesied to you last March about what the year would bring?) as being involved in Germany's fate, as I was resolved to be. I don't look back on the past and accept the present reproachfully, but I don't want the machinations of men to make me waver. All we can do is to live in assurance and faith – you out there with the soldiers, and I in my cell. – I've just come across this in the *Imitation of Christ*: *Custodi diligenter cellam tuam, et custodiet te* ('Take good care of your cell, and it will take care of you'). – May God keep us in faith.

22 December 1943
Letters and Papers from Prison, 174f.

Dimensions of suffering

This is my second Passiontide here. When people suggest in their letters . . . that I'm 'suffering' here, I reject the thought. It seems to me a profanation. These things mustn't be dramatized. I doubt very much whether I'm 'suffering' any more than you, or most people, are suffering today. Of course, a great deal here is horrible, but where isn't it? Perhaps we've made too much of this question of suffering, and been too solemn about it. I've sometimes been surprised that the Roman Catholics take so little notice of that kind of thing. Is it because they're stronger than we are? Perhaps they know better from their own history what suffering and martyrdom really are, and are silent about petty inconveniences and obstacles. I believe, for instance, that physical sufferings, actual pain and so on, are certainly to be classed as 'suffering'. We so like to stress spiritual suffering; and yet that is just what Christ is supposed to have taken from us, and I can find nothing about it in the New Testament, or in the acts of the early martyrs. After all, whether 'the church suffers' is not at all the same as whether one of its servants has to put up with this or that. I think we need a good deal of correction on this point; indeed, I must admit candidly that I sometimes feel almost ashamed of how often we've talked about our own sufferings. No, suffering must be something quite different, and have a quite different dimension, from what I've so far experienced.

9 March 1944
Letters and Papers from Prison, 231f.

Thoughts for a poem

And then at last I should have to start telling you that, in spite of everything that I've written so far, things here are revolting, that my grim experiences often pursue me into the night and that I can shake them off only by reciting one hymn after another, and that I'm apt to wake up with a sigh rather than with a hymn of praise to God. It's possible to get used to physical hardships, and to live for months out of the body, so to speak – almost too much so – but one doesn't get used to the psychological strain; on the contrary, I have the feeling that everything that I see and hear is putting years on me, and I'm often finding the world nauseating and burdensome. You're probably surprised now at my talking like this after all my letters; you wrote very kindly that I was making 'something of an effort' to reassure you about my situation. I often wonder who I really am – the man who goes on squirming under these ghastly experiences in wretchedness that cries to heaven, or the man who scourges himself and pretends to others (and even to himself) that he is placid, cheerful, composed, and in control of himself, and allows people to admire him for it (i.e. for playing the part – or is it not playing a part?). What does one's attitude mean, anyway? In short, I know less than ever about myself, and I'm no longer attaching any importance to it. I've had more than enough psychology, and I'm less and less inclined to analyse the state of my soul. That is why I value Stifter and Gotthelf so much. There is something more at stake than self-knowledge.

15 December 1943
Letters and Papers from Prison, 161f.

Who am I?

Who am I? They often tell me
I would step from my cell's confinement
calmly, cheerfully, firmly,
like a squire from his country-house.

Who am I? They often tell me
I would talk to my warders
freely and friendly and clearly,
as though it were mine to command.

Who am I? They also tell me
I would bear the days of misfortune
equably, smilingly, proudly,
like one accustomed to win.

Am I then really all that which other men tell of?
Or am I only what I know of myself,
restless and longing and sick, like a bird in a cage,
struggling for breath, as though hands were compressing
    my throat,
yearning for colours, for flowers, for the voices of birds,
thirsting for words of kindness, for neighbourliness,
trembling with anger at despotisms and petty humiliation,
tossing in expectation of great events,
powerlessly trembling for friends at an infinite distance,
weary and empty at praying, at thinking, at making,
faint, and ready to say farewell to it all?

Who am I? This or the other?
Am I one person today, and tomorrow another?
Am I both at once? A hypocrite before others,
and before myself a contemptibly woebegone weakling?
Or is something within me still like a beaten army,
fleeing in disorder from victory already achieved?

Who am I? They mock me, these lonely questions of mine.
Whoever I am, thou knowest, O God, I am thine.

Letters and Papers from Prison, 347f.

120

Learning to believe in the life of this world

Dear Eberhard,

All I want to do today is to send you a short greeting. I expect you are often with us here in your thoughts and are always glad of any sign of life, even if the theological discussion stops for a moment. These theological thoughts are, in fact, always occupying my mind; but there are times when I am just content to live the life of faith without worrying about its problems. At those times I simply take pleasure in the day's readings – in particular those of yesterday and today; and I'm always glad to go back to Paul Gerhardt's beautiful hymns.

During the last year or so I've come to know and understand more and more the profound this-worldliness of Christianity. The Christian is not a *homo religiosus*, but simply a man, as Jesus was a man – in contrast, shall we say, to John the Baptist. I don't mean the shallow and banal this-worldliness of the enlightened, the busy, the comfortable, or the lascivious, but the profound this-wordliness, characterized by discipline and the constant knowledge of death and resurrection. I think Luther lived a this-worldly life in this sense.

I remember a conversation that I had in America thirteen years ago with a young French pastor. We were asking ourselves quite simply what we wanted to do with our lives. He said he would like to become a saint (and I think it's quite likely that he did become one). At the time I was very impressed, but I disagreed with him, and said, in effect, that I should like to learn to have faith. For a long time I didn't realize the depth of the contrast. I thought I could acquire faith by trying to live a holy life, or something like it. I suppose I wrote *The Cost of Discipleship* as the end of that path. Today I can see the dangers of that book, though I still stand by what I wrote.

I discovered later, and I'm still discovering right up to this moment, that it is only by living completely in this world that one learns to have faith. One must completely abandon any attempt to make something of oneself, whether it be a saint, or a converted sinner, or a churchman (a so-called priestly type!), a righteous man or an unrighteous one, a sick man or a healthy one. By this-worldliness I mean living unreservedly in life's duties, problems,

121

successes and failures, experiences and perplexities. In so doing we throw ourselves completely into the arms of God, taking seriously, not our own sufferings, but those of God in the world – watching with Christ in Gethsemane. That, I think, is faith; that is *metanoia*; and that is how one becomes a man and a Christian (cf. Jer. 45!). How can success make us arrogant, or failure lead us astray, when we share in God's sufferings through a life of this kind?

I think you see what I mean, even though I put it so briefly. I'm glad to have been able to learn this, and I know I've been able to do so only along the road that I've travelled. So I'm grateful for the past and present, and content with them.

You may be surprised at such a personal letter; but if for once I want to say this kind of thing, to whom should I say it? Perhaps the time will come one day when I can talk to Maria like this; I very much hope so. But I can't expect it of her yet.

May God in his mercy lead us through these times; but above all, may he lead us to himself.

21 July 1944
Letters and Papers from Prison, 369f.

Where is there still room for God?

Anxious souls will ask what room there is left for God now; and as they know of no answer to the question, they condemn the whole development that has brought them to such straits. I wrote to you before about the various emergency exits that have been contrived; and we ought to add to them the *salto mortale* [death-leap] back into the Middle Ages. But the principle of the Middle Ages is heteronomy in the form of clericalism; a return to that can be a counsel of despair, and it would be at the cost of intellectual honesty. It's a dream that reminds one of the song *O wüsst' ich doch den Weg zurück, den weiten Weg ins Kinderland*. There is no such way – at any rate not if it means deliberately abandoning our mental integrity; the only way is that of Matt. 18.3, i.e. through repentance, through *ultimate* honesty.

And we cannot be honest unless we recognize that we have to live in the world *etsi deus non daretur*. And this is just what we do recognize – before God! God himself compels us to recognize it. So our coming of age leads us to a true recognition of our situation before God. God would have us know that we must live as men who manage our lives without him. The God who is with us is the God who forsakes us (Mark 15.34). The God who lets us live in the world without the working hypothesis of God is the God before whom we stand continually. Before God and with God we live without God. God lets himself be pushed out of the world on to the cross. He is weak and powerless in the world, and that is precisely the way, the only way, in which he is with us and helps us. Matt. 8.17 makes it quite clear that Christ helps us, not by virtue of his omnipotence, but by virtue of his weakness and suffering.

Here is the decisive difference between Christianity and all religions. Man's religiosity makes him look in his distress to the power of God in the world: God is the *deus ex machina*. The Bible directs man to God's powerlessness and suffering; only the suffering God can help. To that extent we may say that the development towards the world's coming of age outlined above, which has done away with a false conception of God, opens up a way of seeing the God of the Bible, who wins power and space in the world by his weakness. This will probably be the starting-point for our 'secular interpretation'.

'Christians stand by God in his hour of grieving'; that is what distinguishes Christians from pagans. Jesus asked in Gethsemane. 'Could you not watch with me one hour?' That is a reversal of what the religious man expects from God. Man is summoned to share in God's sufferings at the hands of a godless world.

He must therefore really live in the godless world, without attempting to gloss over or explain its ungodliness in some religious way or other. He must live a 'secular' life, and thereby share in God's sufferings. He *may* live a 'secular' life (as one who has been freed from false religious obligations and inhibitions). To be a Christian does not mean to be religious in a particular way, to make something of oneself (a sinner, a penitent, or a saint) on the basis of some method or other, but to be a man – not a type of man, but the man that Christ creates in us. It is not the religious act that makes the Christian, but participation in the sufferings of

123

God in the secular life. That is *metanoia*: not in the first place thinking about one's own needs, problems, sins, and fears, but allowing oneself to be caught up into the way of Jesus Christ, into the messianic event, thus fulfilling Isa. 53. Therefore 'believe in the gospel', or, in the words of John the Baptist, 'Behold, the Lamb of God, who takes away the sin of the world' (John 1.29). (By the way, Jeremias has recently asserted that the Aramaic word for 'lamb' may also be translated 'servant'; very appropriate in view of Isa. 53!).

This being caught up into the messianic sufferings of God in Jesus Christ takes a variety of forms in the New Testament. It appears in the call to discipleship, in Jesus' table-fellowship with sinners, in 'conversions' in the narrower sense of the word (e.g. Zacchaeus), in the act of the woman who was a sinner (Luke 7) – an act that she performed without any confession of sin, in the healing of the sick (Matt. 8.17; see above), in Jesus' acceptance of children. The shepherds, like the wise men from the East, stand at the crib, not as 'converted sinners', but simply because they are drawn to the crib by the star just as they are. The centurion of Capernaum (who makes no confession of sin) is held up as a model of faith (cf. Jairus). Jesus 'loved' the rich young man. The eunuch (Acts 8) and Cornelius (Acts 10) are not standing at the edge of an abyss. Nathaniel is 'an Israelite indeed, in whom there is no guile' (John 1.47). Finally, Joseph of Arimathea and the women at the tomb. The only thing that is common to all these is their sharing in the suffering of God in Christ. That is their 'faith'. There is nothing of religious method here. The 'religious act' is always something partial; 'faith' is something whole, involving the whole of one's life. Jesus calls men, not to a new religion, but to life.

16 and 18 July 1944
Letters and Papers from Prison, 360f., 361f.

Christians and pagans

1
Men go to God when they are sore bestead,
Pray to him for succour, for his peace, for bread,

For mercy for them sick, sinning, or dead;
All men do so, Christian and unbelieving.

2
Men go to God when he is sore bestead,
Find him poor and scorned, without shelter or bread,
Whelmed under weight of the wicked, the weak, the dead;
Christians stand by God in his hour of grieving.

3
God goes to every man when sore bestead,
Feeds body and spirit with his bread;
For Christians, pagans alike he hangs dead,
And both alike forgiving.

Letters and Papers from Prison, 348f.

Blessing and suffering

You think the Bible hasn't much to say about health, fortune,
vigour, etc. I've been thinking over that again. It's certainly not
true of the Old Testament. The intermediate theological category
between God and human fortune is, as far as I can see, that of
blessing. In the Old Testament – e.g. among the patriarchs –
there's a concern not for fortune, but for God's blessing, which
includes in itself all earthly good. In that blessing the whole of the
earthly life is claimed for God, and it includes all his promises. It
would be natural to suppose that, as usual, the New Testament
spiritualizes the teaching of the Old Testament here, and therefore
to regard the Old Testament blessing as superseded in the New.
But is it an accident that sickness and death are mentioned in
connection with the misuse of the Lord's Supper ('The cup of
blessing', I Cor. 10.16; 11.30), that Jesus restored people's health,
and that while his disciples were with him they 'lacked nothing'?
Now, is it right to set the Old Testament blessing against the cross?
That is what Kierkegaard did. That makes the cross, or at least
suffering, an abstract principle; and that is just what gives rise to
an unhealthy methodism, which deprives suffering of its element
of contingency as a divine ordinance. It's true that in the Old

Testament the person who receives the blessing has to endure a great deal of suffering (e.g. Abraham, Isaac, Jacob, and Joseph), but this never leads to the idea that fortune and suffering, blessing and cross are mutually exclusive and contradictory – nor does it in the New Testament. Indeed, the only difference between the Old and New Testaments in this respect is that in the Old the blessing includes the cross, and in the New the cross includes the blessing.

To turn to a different point: not only action, but also suffering is a way to freedom. In suffering, the deliverance consists in our being allowed to put the matter out of our own hands into God's hands. In this sense death is the crowning of human freedom. Whether the human deed is a matter of faith or not depends on whether we understand our suffering as an extension of our action and a completion of freedom. I think that is very important and very comforting.

Letters and Papers from Prison, 374f.

In him

Once again I've taken up the readings and meditated on them. The key to everything is the 'in him'. All that we may rightly expect from God, and ask him for, is to be found in Jesus Christ. The God of Jesus Christ has nothing to do with what God, as we imagine him, could do and ought to do. If we are to learn what God promises, and what he fulfils, we must persevere in quiet meditation on the life, sayings, deeds, sufferings, and death of Jesus. It is certain that we may always live close to God and in the light of his presence, and that such living is an entirely new life for us; that nothing is then impossible for us, because all things are possible with God; that no earthly power can touch us without his will, and that danger and distress can only drive us closer to him. It is certain that we can claim nothing for ourselves, and may yet pray for everything; it is certain that our joy is hidden in suffering, and our life in death; it is certain that in all this we are in a fellowship that sustains us. In Jesus God has said Yes and Amen to it all, and that Yes and Amen is the firm ground on which we stand.

In these turbulent times we repeatedly lose sight of what really makes life worth living. We think that, because this or that person is living, it makes sense for us to live too. But the truth is that if this earth was good enough for the man Jesus Christ, if such a man as Jesus lived, then, and only then, has life a meaning for us. If Jesus had not lived, then our life would be meaningless, in spite of all the other people whom we know and honour and love. Perhaps we now sometimes forget the meaning and purpose of our profession. But isn't this the simplest way of putting it? The unbiblical idea of 'meaning' is indeed only a translation of what the Bible calls 'promise'.

Please don't ever get anxious or worried about me, but don't forget to pray for me – I'm sure you don't! I am so sure of God's guiding hand that I hope I shall always be kept in that certainty. You must never doubt that I'm travelling with gratitude and cheerfulness along the road where I'm being led. My past life is brim-full of God's goodness, and my sins are covered by the forgiving love of Christ crucified. I'm most thankful for the people I have met, and I only hope that they never have to grieve about me, but that they, too, will always be certain of, and thankful for, God's mercy and forgiveness.

21 and 23 August 1944
Letters and Papers from Prison, 391, 393

Be blessed, world created by God

Ps. 34.20: Many are the afflictions of the righteous, but the Lord delivers him out of them all.

I Peter 3.9: Do not return evil for evil or reviling for reviling, but on the contrary bless, for to this you have been called, that you may obtain a blessing.

The just man suffers under the world; the unjust man does not. The just man suffers under things which others take for granted and find necessary. The just man suffers under injustice, the meaninglessness and perversity of what happens in the world: he suffers under the destruction of the divine ordinances of marriage

127

and family. He suffers not only because he finds this a privation, but also because he recognizes something ungodly in it. The world says, 'That's the way things are; they always have been and they always will be.' The just man says, 'It should not be like that: it's against God.' One can recognize the just man above all from the fact that he suffers in the world. To some degree he acts as God's detector in the world; therefore he suffers as God suffers under the world. 'But the Lord delivers him' – God's help is not to be found in all human suffering. However, God's help is always in the suffering of the righteous, because he suffers with God. God is always there. The just man knows that God allows him to suffer in such a way that he can learn to love God for his own sake. The just man can find God in suffering. That is his help. Find God in your separation and you will find help.

The answer of the just man to the suffering that the world imposes on him is to bless. That was God's answer to the world which nailed Christ to the cross: to bless. God does not compare like with like, nor should the just man. He should not condemn, nor rebuke, but bless. The world would have no hope were this not the case. The world lives by God's blessing and the blessing of the righteous, and it has a future. To bless, that is, to lay hands on something and say: despite everything you belong to God. That is what we do with the world which causes us such suffering. We do not abandon it; we do not reject it, despise it or condemn it, but we summon it to God, we give it hope. We lay hands on it and say: God's blessing be upon you; may he renew you; be blessed, world created by God, for you belong to your creator and redeemer. We have received God's blessing in joy and in suffering. But the one who has himself been blessed cannot but hand it on to others; he must be a blessing where he is. The world can only be renewed by the impossible; and this impossible is God's blessing.

8 June 1934
Predigten II, 466f.

IV · DEATH

Introduction

We find the first echo of Bonhoeffer's poem 'Stations on the Road to Freedom' in Eberhard Bethge's reply of 26 August 1944; 'There is no greater self-sacrifice, no better way of signifying an otherwise unattainable nearness than in a poem . . . It's splendid to see how whole complexes of shared experiences, insights and convictions are aroused in such strophes . . . Most striking and least comprehensible to me so far is the thought of the fourth' (*Letters and Papers from Prison*, 395).

That description, 'least comprehensible', probably still applies today. And that is connected with the fact that here the significance attributed to death takes us beyond the bounds of what can be expressed. So death can be spoken of only in hints. Or in identifications, of the kind that Bonhoeffer attempted in the two autobiographical poems 'The Death of Moses' and 'Jonah'.

> I fail, and sink in thine eternity,
> but see my people marching forward, free.
> Enough that I have borne its shame and sin
> and seen salvation – now I need not live
> ('The Death of Moses', in *Prayers from Prison*, 34).

So too we can probably no more than glimpse that death is the 'greatest of feasts on the journey to freedom eternal'. It is a pity that there is not enough room in this collection for the inclusion of the two poems on Moses and Jonah since they belong among Bonhoeffer's attempts to give unconditional meaning to death. However, 'Jonah' is included in *Letters and Papers from Prison*, and both can be found in the collection made by J. C. Hampe, entitled *Prayers from Prison*.

The selections included in this chapter come from very different times and occasions. They extend from quite ordinary Christian comments on death (as in the London sermon on Wisdom 3.3) to the highly sophisticated comparison between the death that comes to us from outside and the inner death which we have to die daily, though the two have an intrinsic connection.

In all the phases of his life Bonhoeffer was intensively preoccupied with death, even in his early youth – often with no apparent reason. When such reasons began to accumulate, he had long been used to thinking about death. Wherever he encountered it, especially in the frequent news of the deaths of his soldier pupils and friends, he could therefore bring deep comfort. And when he had to face up to his own death after 20 July 1944, he preserved the tranquillity that overcomes death which he had gained through belief in the resurrection of Christ. The last word we have from him could not be anything but, 'It is the end, for me the beginning of life.' He said this to his fellow-prisoner Payne Best, when in Schönberg, in the Bavarian forest, he was summoned from the transport which had already been earmarked for taking prisoners to freedom, to be murdered at Flossenbürg.

The reader will note within the passages selected here a drift which I have already indicated. This is connected with a clear shift of accent in Bonhoeffer's understanding of the resurrection of Christ. It becomes less and less a redemption from the world and its tribulations and suffering, and more and more a liberation for life in the world. Who could fail to recognize the impulses towards life, work and hope in the world which have come – and will continue to come – from Bonhoeffer? His life and work have brought about the rehabilitation of a particular kind of historical optimism related to the world which is hard to shake. The beginning and end of this last chapter provide two particularly fine examples of living from the resurrection of Christ and looking towards resurrection: the poem 'Powers of Good', which is rightly loved throughout the world, and the less well-known but no less beautiful remarks on Ps. 119.19: 'I am a sojourner on earth'.

O.D.

I am a sojourner on earth

I am a sojourner on earth. By that I recognize that I cannot abide here, that my time is short. Nor do I have rights here to possessions or a home. I must receive with gratitude all the good that befalls me, but I must suffer injustice and violence without anyone interceding for me. I have no firm footing either among people or among things. As a guest I am subject to the laws of the place where I am staying. The earth which feeds me has a right to my labour and my strength. It is not for me to despise the earth on which I have my life. I owe it loyalty and gratitude. I may not escape my fate of having to be a sojourner and a stranger, so I may not escape the call of God into this role of being an alien, by dreaming away my earthly life with thoughts of heaven. There can be a very ungodly homesickness for the other world which is certainly not promised a cure. I am to be a sojourner with all that that implies. I am not to close my heart to the tasks, the sorrows and the joys of earth so that I have no part in them, and I am to wait patiently for the fulfilment of the divine promise. However, I really am to wait, and not snatch it in advance through wishes and dreams. Not a word is said here about our home. I know that this earth cannot be our home, and yet I also know that this is God's earth and that even on this earth I am not only a sojourner, but God's pilgrim and alien (Ps. 39.13). But because I am nothing but a sojourner on earth, with no rights, no support and no security; because God himself has made me so weak and insignificant, he has given me one firm pledge of my goal: his word. He will not take this one security from me; he will keep this word with me, and by it he will allow me to feel my strength. Where the word is with me from the beginning, I can find my way in a strange land, my justice in injustice, my support in uncertainty, my strength in work, patience in suffering.

1939/40
Predigten II, 431f.

Death has again come among us, and we must think about it, whether we want to or not. Two things have become important to me recently: death is outside us, and it is in us. Death from outside is the fearful foe which comes to us when it will. It is the man with the scythe, under whose stroke the blossoms fall. It guides the bullet that goes home. We can do nothing against it, 'it has power from the supreme God'. It is the death of the whole human race, God's wrath and the end of all life. But the other is death in us, it is our own death. That too has been in us since the fall of Adam. But it belongs to us. We die daily to it in Jesus Christ or we deny him. This death in us has something to do with love towards Christ and towards men. We die to it when we love Christ and the brethren from the bottom of our hearts, for love is total surrender to what a man loves. This death is grace and the consummation of love. It should be our prayer that we die this death, that it be sent to us, that death only comes to us from outside when we have been made ready for it by this our own death. For our death is really only the way to the perfect love of God.

When fighting and death exercise their wild dominion around us, then we are called to bear witness to God's love and God's peace not only by word and thought, but also by our deeds. Read James 4.1ff.! We should daily ask ourselves where we can bear witness in what we do to the kingdom in which love and peace prevail. The great peace for which we long can only grow again from peace between twos and threes. Let us put an end to all hate, mistrust, envy, disquiet, wherever we can. 'Blessed are the peacemakers, for they shall be called the children of God.'

The Way to Freedom, 254f.

Who understands the choice?

Who understands the choice of those whom God takes to himself early? Does it not seem to us again and again in the early deaths of Christians as though God were robbing himself of his best instruments at a time when he needed them most? But God makes no mistakes. Does God perhaps need our brothers for some hidden service for us in the heavenly world? We should restrain our human thoughts, which always seek to know more than they can, and keep to what is certain. God has loved anyone whom he has called. 'For his soul was pleasing to the Lord, therefore he took him quickly from the midst of wickedness' (Wisd. 4.14). We know that God and the Devil are locked together in combat over the world and that the Devil has a word to say even at death. In the face of death we cannot say in a fatalistic way, 'It is God's will'; we must add the opposite: 'It is not God's will.' Death shows that the world is not what it should be, but that it needs redemption. Christ alone overcomes death. Here, 'It is God's will' and 'It is not God's will' come to the most acute paradox and balance each other out. God agrees to be involved in something that is not his will, and from now on death must serve God despite itself. From now on, 'It is God's will' also embraces 'It is not God's will'. God's will is the overcoming of death through the death of Jesus Christ. Only in the cross and resurrection of Jesus Christ has death come under God's power, must it serve the purpose of God. Not a fatalistic surrender, but living faith in Jesus Christ, who died and has risen again for us, can seriously make an end of death for us.

In life with Jesus Christ, death as a universal fate which comes to us from outside is contrasted with death from within, one's own death, the free death of dying daily with Jesus Christ. Anyone who lives with Christ dies daily to his own will. Christ in us gives us over to death so that he can live in us. So our inner dying grows up against death from the outside. In this way, the Christian accepts his real death; physical death in the true sense does not become the end, but the consummation of life with Jesus Christ. Here we enter the community of the one who could say at his death, 'It is accomplished.'

Dear brothers, it may be that you now have little time or inclination for such thoughts. There are times in which all reality is so mysterious and oppresses us so much that any direct word seems to destroy the mystery of God for us, that we speak about and would like to hear about the last things only in hints. Everything that we can say about our belief then seems so flat and empty against the reality which we experience and behind which we believe there is an unspeakable mystery. It is the same with

133

those of you at the front as it is with us at home: whatever is uttered vanishes in a flash, all formulas no longer make contact with reality. There can be something very real in all this, as long as one word does not vanish within us, namely the name of Jesus Christ. This name remains a word, the word around which we gather all our words. In this word alone lies clarity and strength. 'Within my heart abiding, thy name and cross alone my every thought are guiding, to bring me to thy throne.'

True Patriotism, 124f.

An obituary

Jer. 17.10: I the Lord search the mind and try the heart, to give to every man according to his ways, according to the fruit of his doings.

Rev. 1.14: His eyes were like a flame of fire.

Dear Brother Vibrans,

At the time when our thoughts turn to the passion of our Lord Jesus Christ, in which we attempt to bring under the cross of Christ the universal sorrow that will not let us go, God has sent you and us great personal suffering. The death of your dear son Gerhard has also affected me – more deeply than the news of any other death during this war. I believe that the grief and feeling of emptiness which his death leaves behind in me could hardly have been different had he been my own brother. Gerhard was particularly close to my heart. I have become poorer through his death. How much more true that must be for you, who knew him so much better, and who therefore know so much more clearly what you have lost with him. And how unimaginably hard is Gerhard's death on his young wife, his brothers and sisters, and on Eberhard. Since I came to know Gerhard – and I thank God that I did get to know him – I have become aware that he was a man in a million, and the closer we came together, the more I respected him. With his honesty, his love of the truth, his unselfishness, his purity, he meant more to me personally than I can say, and more than he knew. The combination of simplicity and maturity brought him the trust that he found in a quite

134

exceptional way wherever he went. He was strict in his demands on himself and yet never Pharisaic; he had a cheerful disposition and yet knew all the distress and temptation, the divided character of the human heart. I will remain grateful to him for two things all my life: for showing me the way in which he kept Sunday and for teaching me Claudius' hymn, 'I thank God and rejoice . . .' Both these things have become living possessions to me because of him.

In the seminary Gerhard was good with his fellow brothers. He offered not only his heart but his hand to anyone who needed it. Here he was always drawn to those who were in special need of help. Out of a chivalrous love, above all he stood by the weak and the difficult. Gerhard was always ready to learn, yet in everything he remained himself. Therefore whatever he said and did was always authentic. When I looked at the daily reading for 3 February (Jer. 17.10; Rev. 1.14) after the news of his death, at first I recoiled at its fearful earnestness. But then I understood that both the texts could particularly apply to him. He was always in deadly earnest that faith had to bring forth fruits, that faith could not be without works. He always had the holy judge before his eyes. One could not but trace in his being the fact that the eyes of the one whose gaze is like a flame of fire were upon him. It was that purifying, consuming, cleansing fire which found a reflection in his love of truth and in his unselfishness. So I can read these words on the day of his death with great gratitude and confidence.

Now we must give up all our links with him. In order that under the cross under which he lived and found grace we may act with all our hearts, in great gratitude, and in undivided love for God. In order that we may no longer be concerned for him. In him God has done all things well, and he is at peace. May we too find peace under the cross. May God send us all peace and let us celebrate a joyful Easter after this passiontide . . .

1 March 1942
Gesammelte Schriften II, 590ff.

Life fulfilled

Psalm 90: 'Lord, thou hast been our refuge from one generation to another. Before the mountains were brought forth, or ever the earth and the world were made, thou art God from everlasting, and world without end. Thou turnest man to destruction: again thou sayest, Come again, ye children of men. For a thousand years in thy sight are but as yesterday, seeing that is past as a watch in the night. As soon as thou scatterest them they are even as a sleep, and fade away suddenly like the grass. In the morning it is green, and groweth up, but in the evening it is cut down, dried up, and withered. For we consume away in thy displeasure: and are afraid at thy wrathful indignation. Thou hast set our misdeeds before thee: and our secret sins in the light of thy countenance. For when thou art angry all our days are gone: we bring our years to an end as a tale that is told. The days of our age are threescore years and ten; and though men be so strong that they come to fourscore years, yet is their strength then but labour and sorrow; so soon passeth it away, and we are gone. But who regardeth the power of thy wrath? For even thereafter as a man feareth, so is thy displeasure. So teach us to number our days that we may apply our hearts unto wisdom. Turn thee again, O Lord, at the last: and be gracious unto thy servants. O satisfy us with thy mercy, and that soon: so shall we rejoice and be glad all the days of our life. Comfort us again now after the time that thou hast plagued us, and for the years wherein we have suffered adversity. Shew thy servants thy work and their children thy glory. And the glorious Majesty of the Lord our God be upon us; prosper thou the work of our hands upon us, O prosper thou our handy-work.'

In great gratitude we stand here today at the grave of our dear grandmother who has fallen asleep. God's hand has been kind to us, by leaving her with us until now. We cannot think of our own lives without thinking of hers. She belongs to us completely, and she always will. And God's hand was also kind to her to the end. He did not leave her alone. He allowed her to see children, grandchildren and great-grandchildren. And even in the midst of her last serious illness he allowed her to be cheerful and healthy for a few days so that she could celebrate Christmas again with the whole family, as she had for all the years before. She was able to join in everything with great clarity and love right to the end, and that moved all of us – the family and those who ministered to her. She asked after all those around her, and had good thoughts and wishes for all of them. God also granted her the clarity to see her condition and the strength to face up to it. And if we are sad today that she is no longer with us, we should never forget how grateful we must be.

'Lord, thou hast been our refuge.' In a life as long as hers there are times when one has to learn that we need a refuge. At an early age she lost her father; she had to give up two sons as children and three grandsons died in the war; in her old age things became quieter around her when grandfather died, when her brothers and sisters passed away, and, most recently, when our dear Uncle Otto, her eldest son, left us. God often intervened tangibly in her life; so she had to keep learning what she had known from her childhood onwards: 'Lord, thou hast been our refuge from one generation to another. Before the mountains were brought forth, or ever the earth and the world were made, thou art God from everlasting, and world without end.' She kept to that in her illness, too. Yielding to the will of God, bearing what he puts upon us, facing the facts clearly and looking reality in the eye; doing what needs to be done and has to be done; and silently and uncomplainingly putting up with things when no one else can help, in all things preserving a great inner cheerfulness and strong affirmation of life – this is how she viewed life and how she lived it; this is how she died; and this is how we have loved her.

'Thou turnest man to destruction: again thou sayest, Come again, ye children of men.' She was able to see this coming again in three generations, and that was her greatest joy in life. For her children, grandchildren and great-grandchildren she was always there; she always had time, repose and good advice for everyone. And although she could make the experiences of others her own and feel for them, she passed judgment and gave advice in a very detached way, with an incomparable knowledge of all human affairs and a great love. And while in this way she saw the generations come and grow, she herself became ready to go. In all her experience and wisdom one felt that she was held up by a humble knowledge of the limits of all human knowledge, judgment and life. 'For a thousand years in thy sight are but as

137

yesterday, seeing that is past as a watch in the night.' 'The days of our age are threescore years and ten; and though men be so strong that they come to fourscore years, yet is their strength then but labour and sorrow.' She lived to be ninety-three years old and she passed on to us a legacy from another age. With her passing there passes away a world which we all carry in ourselves in some way and indeed want to carry in ourselves. The immutability of what is right, the free word of the free man, the binding character of a word once given, clarity and matter-of-factness in speech, honesty and simplicity in personal and public life – that was what meant everything to her. That is what she lived by. She experienced in her own life that it was hard work to realize these aims herself. She was not afraid of that hard work. She could not bear to see the rights of others violated. For that reason her last years were troubled by the great suffering brought her by the fate of the Jews among our people, whose burdens she bore and whose suffering she shared. She came from another time, another cultural world – and this world does not go with her into the grave. This heritage, for which we thank her, is our obligation.

We should learn a lesson not only from her life but also from her death. 'So teach us to number our days that we may apply our hearts unto wisdom.' Even such a life, so filled with meaning, so aware, stands under the law of death which is a burden on all human beings. One day we too will have to go, with all our ideals, our aims and our work. Being wise means being aware of our limitations, our end, and far more, being aware of what lies beyond these limitations: the God who is from eternity to eternity, into whose hands we fall, whether we want to or not, in whose hands she has now been taken up into eternity. What are we to say of such a rich and fulfilled life? We call to the God who is our refuge, to whom we can flee in all distress and sorrow: Jesus Christ, in whom is all truth, all righteousness, all freedom and all love. We call on the God who has overcome all hate, all lovelessness, all unquiet through his unconquerable love on the cross of Jesus Christ. We pray that she may see in eternity what here remains concealed and hidden under sin and death, that in peace and clarity she may look on the eternal countenance of God in Jesus Christ.

138

Beginning and end, Lord, are thine,
the life lived between them was mine.
Though lost and in darkness I happen to roam,
with thee, Lord, is brightness, and light is thy home.

And now we must stop being sorrowful. That was not her way. She never wanted to make people sad. We must go back to our work and our daily tasks. She knew that and wanted it. Above all else she loved action and daily work. So we should go from her grave strengthened. Strengthened by her image, her life and death, but strengthened far more by the faith in God who is her and our refuge from generation to generation, strengthened through Jesus Christ. 'And the glorious Majesty of the Lord our God be upon us; prosper thou the work of our hands upon us, O prosper thou our handy-work. Amen.'

15 January 1936
Predigten II, 48–52

Death transformed

Where those of us who are left behind see nothing but distress and anxiety and pain and self-reproaches and regret; where we see nothing but hopelessness and a void, God says, 'But they are at peace.'

God's 'but' goes against all our thinking and searching. It is God's 'but' that does not let the dead die, that raises them and brings them to him. God's 'but' makes death a sleep from which we wake up in a new world. God's 'but' brings the dead to paradise. 'Truly, I say to you, today you will be with me in Paradise' (Luke 23.43), says Christ to the thief who repents as he hangs next to him on the cross. 'But' they are at peace – that means that this is truly not something that can be taken for granted but is something utterly new, absolutely ultimate, something that God brings to pass. Not our peace, but God's peace. However, once again it must be said: there is no room for selfish questioning here, but all our knowledge and all our hope comes only from looking to God, in whose hands we leave everything and whom we believe because he says, 'I am the resurrection and the life' (John 11.25). 'Because I live, you will live also' (John 14.19).

And now we cannot hear of this world of God which is not our world, of the kingdom of peace to which our dead have gone before us, without an immeasurable longing, an indescribable homesickness creeping over us for that world, as it creeps over children at the Christmas crib, in a joy that will become fullness and blessed peace. The one who has never believed in God and his kingdom, who has not yet sensed anything of the kingdom of resurrection, is not homesick from this time on, nor does he wait, wait joyfully for the redemption of the body.

Whether we are young or old makes no difference here. What are twenty or thirty or fifty years before God. And who knows how near he may already be to the end? Both young and old should reflect that life only begins when it ends here, that all this is only an overture before closed curtains. So why are we so anxious in thinking about death? Why are we so sad when we imagine ourselves lying on our deathbed? Death is only fearful for the one who is anxious, who fears it. Death is not wild and terrible, provided that we are still and hold to God's word. Death is not bitter if we are not embittered. Death is grace, God's greatest grace, which he sends to those who believe in him. Death is gentle, death is sweet, death is soft, death calls us with heavenly power provided that we know that it is the gateway to our home, to the tent of joy, to the eternal realm of peace.

Perhaps we might say: I'm not afraid of death but I am afraid of dying. Who knows that dying is something terrible? Who knows whether the anxiety and distress of men and women is not just trembling and shuddering before the most glorious, most heavenly, most blessed event in the world? Whether it is not the struggling of the newborn child who looks on the light of day? What are all the remarkable things that we can experience at deathbeds if not an indication of this? What does it mean for someone who has fought and struggled long, with great anxiety, at the last moment to open his eyes wide, as though he could see something splendid, and cry out, 'God, that's beautiful!' We have to ask: What does that mean?

Yes, death is certainly terrible. It is the skeleton with the scythe which summons people one after another to the dance of death, whether they will or not – if someone does not believe, if he is not one of the righteous, of whom it is said, 'But they are in peace.'

Death is hell and night and cold if our faith does not transform it. But that is the marvellous thing, that we can transform death. When our faith in God touches it, then the wild skeleton who terrifies us becomes the friend, the messenger of God. Then death itself becomes Christ. Yes, these are very hidden things. But we may know them. And our life depends on them. Those who believe will have peace, and death will not terrify them. It can no longer touch them, for they are in the hand of God and no torment touches them.

Some people have tried to make death a friend. And then death has failed them in their last hours, and become an enemy. There is only one way to have death as a friend, and that is faith. Then death becomes our best friend. Then God's word will ring out once again over our deathbed: 'But they are in peace.' And our eyes will open wide for joy, when we see this kingdom and this peace.

Perhaps it may seem childish to you that we talk like this. But can we be other than childish in this way in the face of such things? In the face of such things are we really ever other than children, unsuspecting children? And would we want to be anything else if we are allowed to come into his kingdom and see the day of joy. Look at your children when they are happy. And ask yourself whether there is anything you would rather see. Should we be ashamed of this? 'As one whom his mother comforts, I will comfort you' (Isa. 66.13).

Christ called us children of the resurrection. We are homesick children, if all goes well with us.

26 November 1934
Predigten I, 398–401

'I'll bring again'

For this last week or so these lines have kept on running through my head:

> Let pass, dear brothers, every pain;
> What you have missed I'll bring again.

What does this 'I'll bring again' mean? It means that nothing is lost, that everything is taken up in Christ, although it is transformed, made transparent, clear, and free from all selfish desire. Christ restores all this as God originally intended it to be, without the distortion resulting from our sins. The doctrine derived from Eph. 1.10 – that of the restoration of all things, ἀνακεφαλαίωσις, *recapitulatio* (Irenaeus) – is a magnificent conception, full of comfort. This is how the promise 'God seeks what has been driven away' is fulfilled. And no one has expressed this so simply and artlessly as Paul Gerhardt in these words that he puts into the mouth of the Christ-child: 'I'll bring again'. Perhaps this line will help you a little in the coming weeks. Besides that, I've lately learnt for the first time to appreciate the hymn 'Beside thy cradle here I stand'. Up to now I hadn't made much of it; I suppose one has to be alone for a long time, and meditate on it, to be able to take it in properly. Every word is remarkably full of meaning and beauty. There's just a slight flavour of the monastery and mysticism, but no more than is justified. After all, it's right to speak of 'I' and 'Christ' as well as of 'we', and what that means can hardly be expressed better than it is in this hymn. There are also a few passages in a similar vein in the *Imitation of Christ*, which I'm reading now and then in the Latin (it reads much better in Latin than in German); and sometimes think of

from the Augustinian *O bone Jesu* by Schütz. Doesn't this passage, in its ecstatic longing combined with pure devotion, suggest the 'bringing again' of all earthly desire? 'Bringing again' mustn't, of course, be confused with 'sublimation'; 'sublimation' is σάρξ 'flesh' (and pietistic?), and 'restoration' is spirit, not in the sense of 'spiritualization' (which is also σάρξ), but of καινὴ κτίσις through the πνεῦμα ἅγιον, a new creation through the Holy Spirit. I think this point is also very important when we have to talk to people who ask us about their relation to their dead. '*I* will bring again' – that is, we cannot and should not take it back ourselves, but allow Christ to give it back to us. (By the way, I should like the choir to sing at my funeral 'One thing

I desire of the Lord', 'Hasten, God, to deliver me', and *O bone Jesu*.)

Letters and Papers from Prison, 169ff.

The joy of the one who overcomes

'With everlasting joy upon their heads . . .' (Isa. 35.10). We do not grudge it them; indeed, should we say that sometimes we envy them in the stillness? Since ancient times, *accidie* – sorrowfulness of the heart, 'resignation' – has been one of the deadly sins. 'Serve the Lord with gladness' (Ps. 100.2) summons us to the scriptures. This is what our life has been given to us for, what it has been preserved for up till now. Joy belongs, not only to those who have been called home, but also to the living, and no one shall take it from us. We are one with them in this joy, but never in sorrow. How shall we be able to help those who have become joyless and fearful unless we ourselves are supported by courage and joy? I don't mean by this something fabricated, compelled, but something given, free. Joy dwells with God; it descends from him and seizes spirit, soul and body, and where this joy has grasped a man it grows greater, carries him away, opens closed doors. There is a joy which knows nothing of sorrow, need and anxiety of the heart; it has no duration, and it can only drug one for the moment. The joy of God has been through the poverty of the crib and the distress of the cross; therefore it is insuperable, irrefutable. It does not deny the distress where it is, but finds God in the midst of it, indeed precisely there; it does not contest the most grievous sin, but finds forgiveness in just this way; it looks death in the face, yet finds life in death itself. We are concerned with this joy which has overcome. It alone is worth believing, it alone helps and heals. The joy of our friends who have been called home is also the joy of those who have overcome – the risen one bears the marks of the cross upon his body; we are still engaged in conflict daily, they have overcome for all time. God alone knows how near to us or far from us stands the last overcoming, in which our own death can become joy. 'With peace and joy I go hence . . .'

True Patriotism, 189

We live in the next to last and believe in the last

My thoughts and feelings seem to be getting more and more like those of the Old Testament, and in recent months I have been reading the Old Testament much more than the New. It is only when one knows the unutterability of the name of God that one can utter the name of Jesus Christ; it is only when one loves life and the earth so much that without them everything seems to be over that one may believe in the resurrection and a new world; it is only when one submits to God's law that one may speak of grace; and it is only when God's wrath and vengeance are hanging as grim realities over the heads of one's enemies that something of what it means to love and forgive them can touch our hearts. In my opinion it is not Christian to want to take our thoughts and feelings too quickly and too directly from the New Testament. We have already talked about this several times, and every day confirms my opinion. One cannot and must not speak the last word before the last but one. We live in the last but one and believe the last, don't we? Lutherans (so-called!) and pietists would shudder at the thought, but it is true all the same. In *The Cost of Discipleship* (ch. 1) I just hinted at this, but did not follow it up; I must do so later. But the logical conclusions are far-reaching.

Letters and Papers from Prison, 156f.

Directed to the earth by resurrection

Now for some further thoughts about the Old Testament. Unlike the other oriental religions, the faith of the Old Testament isn't a religion of redemption. It's true that Christianity has always been regarded as a religion of redemption. But isn't this a cardinal error, which separates Christ from the Old Testament and interprets him on the lines of the myths about redemption? To the objection that a crucial importance is given in the Old Testament to redemption (from Egypt, and later from Babylon – cf. Deutero-Isaiah) it may be answered that the redemptions referred to here are *historical*, i.e. on *this* side of death, whereas everywhere else the myths about redemption are concerned to overcome the barrier of death. Israel is delivered out of Egypt so that it may live before

God as God's people on earth. The redemption myths try unhistorically to find an eternity after death. Sheol and Hades are no metaphysical constructions, but images which imply that the 'past', while it still exists, has only a shadowy existence in the present.

The decisive factor is said to be that in Christianity the hope of resurrection is proclaimed, and that that means the emergence of a genuine religion of redemption, the main emphasis now being on the far side of the boundary drawn by death. But it seems to me that this is just where the mistake and the danger lie. Redemption now means redemption from cares, distress, fears, and longings, from sin and death, in a better world beyond the grave. But is this really the essential character of the proclamation of Christ in the gospels and by Paul? I should say it is not. The difference between the Christian hope of resurrection and the mythological hope is that the former sends a man back to his life on earth in a wholly new way which is even more sharply defined than it is in the Old Testament. The Christian, unlike the devotees of the redemption myths, has no last line of escape available from earthly tasks and difficulties into the eternal, but, like Christ himself ('My God, why hast thou forsaken me?'), he must drink the earthly cup to the dregs, and only in his doing so is the crucified and risen Lord with him, and he crucified and risen with Christ. This world must not be prematurely written off; in this the Old and New Testaments are at one. Redemption myths arise from human boundary-experiences, but Christ takes hold of a man at the centre of his life.

Letters and Papers from Prison, 336f.

Coping with death

Perhaps I already ought to be sending you my special good wishes for Easter, as I don't know how long it takes for letters to reach you and I would very much like you to know that in the weeks before and after Easter I know that I'm one with you in many good memories. In looking through *Das Neue Lied* these days, I'm constantly reminded that it is mainly to you that I owe my enjoyment of the Easter hymns. It's a year now since I heard a hymn sung. But it's strange how the music that we hear inwardly can almost surpass, if we really concentrate on it, what we hear physically. It has a greater purity, the dross falls away, and in a way the music acquires a 'new body'. There are only a few pieces that I know well enough to be able to hear them inwardly, but I get on particularly well with the Easter hymns . . .

Easter? We're paying more attention to dying than to death. We're more concerned to get over the act of dying than to overcome death. Socrates mastered the art of dying; Christ overcame death as 'the last enemy' (I Cor. 15.26). There is a real difference between the two things; the one is within the scope of human possibilities, the other means resurrection. It's not from *ars moriendi*, the art of dying, but from the resurrection of Christ, that a new and purifying wind can blow through our present world. *Here* is the answer to δὸς μοὶ ποῦ στῶ καὶ κινήσω τὴν γῆν. If a few people really believed that and acted on it in their daily lives, a great deal would be changed. To live in the light of the resurrection – that is what Easter means. Do you find, too, that most people don't know what they really live by? This *perturbatio animorum* spreads amazingly. It's an unconscious waiting for the word of deliverance, though the time is probably not yet ripe for it to be heard. But the time will come, and this Easter may be one of our last chances to prepare ourselves for our great task of the future.

Letters and Papers from Prison, 240f.

Powers of good: a letter and a poem

[Prinz-Albrecht-Strasse]
28 December 1944

Dear Mother,

I'm so glad to have just got permission to write you a birthday letter. I have to write in some haste, as the post is just going. All I really want to do is to help to cheer you a little in these days that you must be finding so bleak. Dear mother, I want you to know that I am constantly thinking of you and father every day, and that I thank God for all that you are to me and the whole family. I know you've always lived for us and haven't lived a life of your own. That is why you're the only one with whom I can share all

146

that I'm going through. It's a very great comfort to me that Maria is with you. Thank you for all the love that has come to me in my cell from you during the past year, and has made every day easier for me. I think these hard years have brought us closer together than we ever were before. My wish for you and father and Maria and for us all is that the New Year may bring us at least an occasional glimmer of light, and that we may once more have the joy of being together. May God keep you both well.

With every power for good to stay and guide me,
comforted and inspired beyond all fear,
I'll live these days with you in thought beside me,
and pass, with you, into the coming year.

The old year still torments our hearts, unhastening;
the long days of our sorrow still endure;
Father, grant to the souls thou hast been chastening
that thou hast promised, the healing and the cure.

Should it be ours to drain the cup of grieving
even to the dregs of pain, at thy command,
we will not falter, thankfully receiving
all that is given by thy loving hand.

But should it be thy will once more to release us
to life's enjoyment and its good sunshine,
that which we've learned from sorrow shall increase us,
and all our life be dedicate as thine.

Today, let candles shed their radiant greeting;
lo, on our darkness are they not thy light
leading us, haply, to our longed-for meeting? –
Thou canst illumine even our darkest night.

When now the silence deepens for our hearkening,
grant we may hear thy children's voices raise
from all the unseen world around us darkening
their universal paean, in thy praise.

147

While all the powers of good aid and attend us,
boldly we'll face the future, come what may.
At even and at morn God will befriend us,
and oh, most surely on each newborn day!

Letters and Papers from Prison, 399ff.

Suggestions for further reading

No selection, however carefully made, can be a substitute for wider acquaintance with Bonhoeffer's writing. Because the great variety of the works he left behind presents problems to the reader unfamiliar with them, here are few comments by way of guidance.

Above all else it is important to read a biography. Those who find Eberhard Bethge's great biography, *Dietrich Bonhoeffer, Theologian, Christian, Contemporary*, Collins 1970 too daunting should try Bethge's shorter book, *Bonhoeffer: An Illustrated Introduction*, Collins 1979, or Mary Bonsanquet's *The Life and Death of Dietrich Bonhoeffer*, Hodder 1968.

The easiest approach to Bonhoeffer is by his *Letters and Papers from Prison*. First published in English in 1953 and several times revised, the authorized translation now exists in two versions, both published by SCM Press: the full version, expanded by Eberhard Bethge, who edited the book, was published in 1971 as The Enlarged Edition; an abridged version was published in 1981. Of all Bonhoeffer's works this is the one which has spoken most directly to a wide public, as it still does. Some writings from prison not included in this book can be found in *Prayers from Prison*, Collins 1977.

Bonhoeffer's short book *Life Together*, SCM Press 1954, is very easy to read. It was, of course, written for a quite specific audience with a quite specific purpose. However, it contains so much that is generally valid that all readers have felt enriched by it.

Bonhoeffer's exposition of the Sermon on the Mount (*The Cost of Discipleship*, SCM Press 1959) is an attempt to answer the question whether the Sermon on the Mount can be a guide for our lives.

Bonhoeffer's fragments on *Ethics* (SCM Press 1955) have become increasingly significant as the years have gone by. Bonhoeffer himself saw the writing of a book on ethics as his real life's work.

149

The most valuable key to the fragments on *Ethics* is the essay 'After Ten Years', which is contained in this book.